KILMAINHAM

Kilmainham

The history of a settlement older than Dublin

with an account of its founder
Saint Maignenn, and of its holy well

Colum Kenny

FOUR COURTS PRESS

Set in 10 on 12 point Bembo
and published by
FOUR COURTS PRESS LTD
Kill Lane, Blackrock, Co. Dublin, Ireland
and in North America by
FOUR COURTS PRESS LTD
c/o ISBS, 5804 NE Hassalo Street, Portland, OR 97213.

A catalogue record for this title
is available from the British Library.

ISBN 1-85182-219-4

Printed in Ireland
by Colour Books Ltd, Dublin.

Contents

Illustrations

The lion-device at the head of each chapter is based on a
fragment of medieval floor-tile found at Kilmainham, 1948.

Preface

In telling the story of a settlement which was first inhabited long before the Vikings founded Dublin, I have touched on the major events and developments which have made Kilmainham what it is today. Also considered below are local phenomena which once were of special significance but which are no longer remembered. These include a mysterious fire which was said to be 'privileged', and the popular holy well of St John.

Kilmainham, County Dublin, takes its name from the chapel of Maignenn, an Irish Christian who is said to have lived in the sixth and seventh centuries. The consecrated precincts of his foundation are marked today by an ancient and enigmatic granite shaft. Nearby, in centuries past, crowds gathered annually at the holy well. By the ninth century, at the latest, the feast of Saint Maignenn of Kilmainham was being celebrated in Ireland on 18 December each year.[1]

Maignenn's chapel, or 'cell', appears to have stood on an elevated site near the western boundary of the present grounds of the Royal Hospital. Before the Liffey and the Camac rivers join near Heuston Station, they run parallel for about a mile. Some 700 yards apart, they enclose a gravel ridge that rises sharply to a height of sixty feet above the banks of the two rivers. On this dominant and isolated plateau, with the sea visible to the east and nearer then than is the present coast-line, Maignenn and his followers lived. Towards the mouth of the River Liffey the city of Dublin would later rise.

Because of his importance as the founder of Kilmainham this history begins with an account of events in the life of Maignenn. The account is based on a manuscript in the British Library.[2] For the first time, in chapter 1, this rare document is examined in some detail and its description of particular incidents is placed within its contemporary context. The old manuscript is referred to in the text below simply as the 'Account'.

Of particular interest in the 'Account' is an intriguing reference to a special fire, which appears once to have been kept burning at Kilmainham. In chapter 2 an attempt is made to understand the significance of this by discussing certain other sacred fires, with one of which Kilmainham was explicitly connected.

In chapter 3 we stand on firmer ground, historically, as the Vikings arrive in Ireland. A growing number of scholars consider it likely that these invaders first seized and settled at Kilmainham before founding the city of Dublin. The strategic importance of Kilmainham, perched as it is on the western approaches to Dublin, was underlined on the eve of the Battle of Clontarf by the decision of Brian Boru to burn the older settlement. This is an unpalatable fact which, hitherto, has received scant attention from historians.

The military significance of Kilmainham was confirmed when the Normans invaded Ireland and the Knights Hospitallers were granted the high ground between the Liffey and the Camac. This is one aspect of the history of Kilmainham which has already been the object of serious study and in chapter 4 we review what is known of the period and contemplate the symbol which was to be seen in the windows of the priory of the knights. We also get a glimpse of life for the ordinary people of Kilmainham in 1305.

Chapter 5 is devoted to a brief consideration of the years between the dissolution of the monasteries and the foundation of the Royal Hospital. During this troubled era in Ireland's history the former priory was used as a centre of government business and from this time the first map of the area survives.

Before moving on to consider events in the modern period, chapters 6 and 7 are devoted respectively to St John's Well and to the celebrations which took place there at midsummer, as well as at certain other times of the year. Members of both the protestant and catholic establishments frowned upon practices associated with this well and attempted to suppress them.

It was not until the nineteenth century that the town of Kilmainham took on a shape which would be familiar to modern readers. The building of a new gaol and court-house on Gallows' Hill were an important magnet for development and shifted the focus locally up from old Kilmainham to the ridge. Incidentally, the spelling 'gaol', rather than 'jail', has been adopted below as it is that which is commonly employed in the context of Kilmainham. The gradual process of industrialisation also ensured a fresh influx of inhabitants to the area. As we see in chapter 8 none of these changes dampened the enthusiasm of those people who liked to visit St John's Well, although that remarkable cemetery known as 'Bully's Acre' was closed down.

Of great significance in the history of Kilmainham were the years when Victoria sat on the throne and, appropriately, we find that she and her husband paid a visit to the Royal Hospital.

During the decades of her reign the new railway line swept aside the old well which managed, nonetheless, to struggle on and to emerge at another outlet surrounded by new devotees. It was at this time too that an act of parliament was passed creating the township of Kilmainham. In Chapter 9 we take our time to consider these and other relevant aspects of 'Victorian progress'.

At the opening of the twentieth century the township was absorbed into the city of Dublin and, with the foundation of a new state, the old men of the Royal Hospital left for England. Having been suggested but rejected as a home for the new national university and, subsequently, as a permanent location for the houses of the Oireachtas, the Royal Hospital went into decline for many decades. In chapter 10 these events are recalled,

The future of both Kilmainham and of its holy well are discussed in a brief Epilogue. The recent restoration of the old Royal Hospital, in the form of the Irish Museum of Modern Art, and the construction of a museum at the gaol indicate a fresh awareness of Kilmainham's heritage.

In preparing this history of Kilmainham, I have had assistance from people at a number of institutions, including the Archdiocese of Dublin, Bibliothèque Nationale de France, Bray Public Library, British Library, Córas Iompair Éireann, Dublin City University, Dublin Corporation, Dublin Institute for Advanced Studies, Fingal County Council, Geological Survey of Ireland, Irish Folklore Commission at University College Dublin, Irish Museum of Modern Art, Kilmainham Gaol, King's Inns Library, National Archives, National Library, National Museum, Office of Public Works, Royal Irish Academy, Royal Society of Antiquaries of Ireland, Samye Trust, Trinity College Dublin and the Valuation Office. The services of these institutions and of their personnel have been greatly appreciated.

In particular, I would like to thank Dr Máirín Ní Dhonnchadha, of the School of Celtic Studies, and Mr John O'Neill of Kilmainham. Dr Ní Dhonnchadha gave very generously of her time to help me to make some sense of the Paris account of Maignenn's life and of the saint's purported genealogy. Any errors which occur in respect of these matters are entirely due to the author's ignorance. Mr O'Neill encouraged me to undertake this study and kindly and critically read a draft of it. I also wish to express my appreciation for the help and support of my wife Catherine and of our children, Oisín, Conor and Samuel.

An account of Saint Maignenn

Maignenn and his three brothers, Librén, Cobthach and Toa, all came to be regarded by the medieval church as saints. Their father Áed was a northerner, who is said to have died in AD 606. Their mother is reputed to have been a sister of Saint Senshincell or 'old Senchell', who was an abbot in the area now known as Co. Offaly. It is unclear to what extent the information which we have relating to the ancestry of Maignenn is reliable. When the administration of monasteries tended to pass from generation to generation of the same family such genealogies, demonstrating a fine lineage, might come to have some material value.[1]

Maignenn was 'abbot of Kilmainham', being thus described in the early martyrologies and elsewhere. That he was also a bishop is suggested in the 'Account' and in a list consulted by the compiler of the 'Martyrology of Christ Church, Dublin'. Such distinctions were not as clear-cut in the early church as they later became and it is possible that Maignenn combined both roles, as indeed is suggested by the 'Martyrology of Donegal' which was compiled from older manuscripts about 1630. There is no record of any diocese of Kilmainham, and none of Dublin before the eleventh century.[2]

Before considering in some detail the 'Account' of Maigenn which is in the British Library, it is necessary to enter a caveat. The medieval biographies of saints need not be taken literally. They often include many fantastic tales and anachronistic elements. Most, like that of Maignenn, reach us only in versions which were written later than the lives of the saints who are described. The 'lives' often include stories which were in circulation from a period much earlier than that in which they were written but scribes were also known to revise and to 'correct' existing histories – as they saw fit. Where folklore meets myth and where both yield to fact or to fiction is difficult to say and we must heed Sharpe's observation that others have approached such accounts in a spirit of discovering something which they wanted to know. Such advice is to be qualified by that of John Ryan who suggested that, 'in dealing with these *Lives*, excessive scepticism and excessive credulity are equally to be eschewed'.[3]

Flower described the 'Account' of Maignenn as 'a homiletic collection of his sayings on matters of discipline, eschatology, etc.' and Kenney regarded the manuscript as 'late and very fabulous'.[4] It is a series of tales about Maignenn and about his encounters and conversations with other holy men. It contains insights into the early church and its controversies, a church in which there was a degree of self-mortification which may seem extreme today. Thus Saint Finnchu(a) of Munster, with whom Maignenn is said to have visited the Aran Islands, 'used to lie the first night with every corpse which used to be buried in his church' and he had a little 'prison' built, not much wider or longer than himself, in which he used to hang by his armpits from iron staples so that his feet could not touch the floor nor his head rest either'.[5]

'LAMB OF COMPASSION'

The 'Account' indicates that Maignenn was recognised as a special person from an early age. Its author tells us that, when the saint was just three years old, the king of Ireland's steward came to demand rent of his nurse – but took 'a thing to which he had no right at all'. The nurse, on whose bosom Maignenn lay, wept with a loud cry and straightaway the steward lost the power of a leg, of an arm and of an eye. The steward 'vociferated', saying

> I saw a dream but lately, as though I had been guilty in the matter of a 'lamb of compassion', which lamb I now deem that child thou hast to be – and, wouldst thou in his name procure me succour of God now, never again henceforth would I lift rent on thee.

The nurse appealed to Maignenn to cure the steward and, raising his hands to God, he did so: 'Indoors there is a clamour and among them all it is reported that Maignenn is a holy child'.

Maignenn is said to have come to be regarded, 'from Shannon to *Benn Edair* [Howth Hill], [as] a river of piety'. From the day of his ordination he 'never uttered a falsehood' and, to avoid temptation, he 'never looked a woman in the face'.

He advised a seven-year-old relation to 'sleep as it were of a captive cast for death' and to pray each night, 'as though that night should be one's last'. He recommended frequent 'meditation on God'. The 'Account' gives what are described as 'some of bishop Maignenn's perfections'. These include five 'meditations' before eating or drinking anything:

> the first of them being how he was born originally, and in how mean estate he came from his mother's womb; the second, how in time he should escape out of his death-extremity; the third, how the soul is rapt away to look on Hell; the fourth again, how it goes to contemplate the Heavenly City that it may shun being taken back again, whereby its self-distrust is all the greater; the fifth, how the sinner's cairn is in a trifling while afterwards abased.

He used to tell his monks that for the Holy Spirit they ought in their inmost parts to leave a passage free: one into which they should not admit secular sustenance. Thrice at a time he was wont to say that the world is a mere mass of deception.

It is said that 'he never entered into any place where war or conflict was but mercifulness and pity would attend that which he said and, before he departed, the parties would be at peace'. He was described as 'Maignenn the wonder-worker, that never sinned with woman; Maignenn the sage, whose use and wont it was to weep'. He had a pet ram which carried his Psalter, as Saint Ciaran had a friendly fox for similar purposes. Often the psalms were inscribed on waxed wooden tablets instead of scarce parchment or vellum. A disconcerting habit which Maignenn had was that 'never was any for three hours in his company but he would reveal what spirit were in him, and would understand speedily whether it were good angel or bad that accompanied any man's body'.[6]

He himself appears to have been troubled by some kind of 'peist', perhaps a gut-worm rather than a psychological demon. In an account, written about the year 800, we are told that

> Fursa once happened to visit Maignenn of Kilmainham and they make their union and exchange their troubles in token of their union, to wit the headache or piles from which Fursa suffered to be on Maignenn, and the reptile that was in Maignenn to enter Fursa. So that it became Fursa's practice every morning always to eat three bits of bacon that he might abate the reptile's violence.[7]

Maignenn engaged in 'malediction'. This practice of praying against another echoed the pre-Christian ritual of cursing. It arises in the 'Account' when a robber steals the cow which belonged to 'the leper woman of Kilmainham' and from whose milk she used to feed those who were poor or 'palsied'. Maignenn is incensed and 'the bells in the place, great and small are rung; and against the robber they with bell, with cursing and malediction, pronounce excommunication'. Nor would he later let any of his people 'afford the thief a prayer or even one sign of compassion'. Maignenn clearly saw some things quite simply. Thus, he petitioned God for

> plenty and honour and worldly wealth to be theirs that should favour his clergy and his representative after him; while to them that should persecute his precinct and his own peculiar see he left three legacies: a life short and transient, blotting out of their posterity, and the Earth not to yield them her fruit.

Some writers attempt to place Maignenn at his monastery in Kilmainham in AD 606, but they appear to be following Archdall, who simply has him flourishing about that year on the basis of his father's date of death in the passage of the *Acta S.S.* quoted in Appendix A below.

Like other members of the learned classes in Gaelic Ireland the monks occasionally made a point of visiting their colleagues. In the 'Account' we find Maignenn on his rounds of devotion meeting a succession of other saints who lived in the sixth and seventh centuries. He apparently lived long enough to have 'studied fervently with Ireland's twelve apostles'.[8]

ROUNDS OF DEVOTION

The first encounter recorded in the 'Account of Maignenn' is with Loman of *Loch Uair* (Lough Owel, Co.Westmeath). In Loman's 'town', or monastic settlement, Maignenn was startled to meet an old friend who 'had been his hearer' but whom he has not seen for thirty years. This friend had failed to follow the saint's counsel and his eyes had become greatly diseased. Maigenn agreed, 'for God's sake, to protect him' and said to him: 'that which thou wouldst take ill to be done to thyself, do not to another, and tho' thou be in thy latter time, yet will God take thee to him'.

1 Folio from the 'Account' of Maignenn (before AD 1500).

Maignenn 'on this occasion' also preached to 'the king of Ireland', Dermot, son of Fergus. He warned of 'the Day of Doom and the rigorous judgements of the Triune God [Holy Trinity]'. The sermon had such an effect on Loman that 'he broke out and wept aloud'. It also moved 'a score and ten' of the king's people who 'in the king's presence ... severed themselves from the false world'. Some of these may have been among the 'thrice nine clerics' or 'knot' who are said later to have accompanied Maignenn on his rounds. The king was so impressed that he assigned to Maignenn various tributes due to himself, including the 'nose-tax'.[9]

Then there was the time Maignenn went to visit Finnian who, 'most probably not later than 540' had founded a church at Maghbile at the head of Strangford Lough in the present Co. Down. As the two men walked out at vespertide,

> they witnessed a linen altar-cloth that with an undulating motion was just come down out of the firmament. Said bishop Maignenn: 'Pick up that, Finnian'. 'Never say it, holy bishop', Finnian answered, 'himself art he whom such doth best befit, nor is the thing a likely one for me to have'. Maignenn the bishop said: 'I swear by the angels that, until from God I have just such another, I will not lift it'. A second time they look up to God, and between them crave yet another altar-cloth [and it was vouchsafed them].[10]

The fifteenth-century reader is told that 'these same linen cloths are in being still'. Another time Maignenn and the 'thrice nine clerics' who were his companions went with Saint Finnchua to visit the Aran Islands, which were at the very western extremity of the known world and 'to which there was resort of Ireland's and indeed of all Europe's saints'.[11] On their way home they found themselves without meat but Maignenn told them to have faith. Soon a deer dropped dead in front of them. When they had eaten Maignenn lectured them on fasting and how it 'profits nought' if fasting is undertaken unwillingly or in the spirit of vanity:

> I tell you also, miserable beings, that for the evil which a man does actually God impleads him not more straitly than he indites him for the good which, when he might have done it, he neglected and performed it not.

On a visit to Moling in the present Co. Carlow he was told of a strange cross and fresh grave at *Bearna na Gaoithe*, which he had passed without noticing. He returned to *Bearna na Gaoithe* and stood silently by the grave for three hours, only moving to bend his knee to the cross three times. Then, 'in a voice mild and gentle', he charged the occupant to identify himself 'and what the reason I never saw the cross, and I after passing close beside it'. The deceased replied, 'I am a heathen, and never was it feasible to do evil but I did it'. He explained that he was excommunicated and that it was Maignenn's guardian angel who had prevented him from seeing the grave. The deceased then asked for mercy but the guardian angel told Maignenn, 'Rouse not God's wrath, neither any more idly waste thy time', and Maignenn departed.[12]

To a simple greeting from Mochuda of Raheen, 'How art thou my friend?', he replied smartly, 'I am not as I have been; and shall be not as I am, and shall yet go to nothing'. The two thereupon fell to discussing 'concubinage of women and of priests', which then as now was a problem for the Irish church. Maignenn had a dire warning for priests and for women who have sexual relations with them. The former have been as guilty as a murderer and the latter have sinned with the equivalent of thousands of men, 'the reason of which is that they be ten legions of angels which accompany the body of every priest that is chaste'. Any man who subsequently goes with that woman is himself 'thrusting a head into mire', is guilty of 'a renunciation of baptism, of faith, of piety' and is making 'a pact with Lucifer'.[13]

Having disposed of concubinage, Mochuda quizzed Maignenn on the subject of pilgrimages, which were an important feature of the early church. Maignenn pointed out that the most important aspect of pilgrimage is right motivation:

> such and such performs a pilgrimage when he finds his heart vehemently incline to pilgrimage, but feebleness or poverty or burden of household care suffers him not to perform it; which then is to him the same as though he visited the tombstones of Peter and of Paul, and Christ's sepulchre.

On his circuit of devotion Maignenn visited Maelruain of Tallaght in order to make confession. He found him 'just emerging out of a well of water after chanting of the Psalter three times fifty psalms in it'. There are shades here of ordeal by water and of the ceremonies which, as we shall see, traditionally surrounded holy wells such as that at Kilmainham. However, standing in a spring was also an obvious form of penance, with its biblical undercurrents of being 'born again of water and the holy spirit'.

Prayer in general and the Psalter, or 'three fifties', in particular played a central role in the Céli Dé reform movement, of which Maelruain was one of the two mainstays. Memorising long tracts was a feature of Gaelic and other cultures in an era before books were common and Maelruain expected his monks to recite all 150 psalms at a time. Across the Liffey at Finglas, the other mainstay of the Céli Dé reform, Dublittir, is known to have recited the entire Psalter while standing, prostrating himself after each psalm. Between these 'two eyes' of the Céli Dé, as the monasteries of Tallaght and Finglas were known, lay Kilmainham.[14]

There was a certain tension between Maignenn and Maelruain relating to the moral obligation to work. While deference was paid by Maelruain to Maignenn, the 'sacred bishop', the former hesitated before hearing the latter's confession because Maignenn no longer engaged in corporal labour, 'respect to my day being had'. So the two discussed the injunction which God laid on man 'to feed himself by his hand's and by his body's labour, and with his sweat'. Any initial difficulty was overcome and Maelruain went on to predict of Maignenn that 'sages and ancient books [shall] have preserved to the World's end thy journey hither [and] to thy see great prerogatives shall belong'. He also, as we shall see, predicted a special privilege for 'Maignenn's fire in Kilmainham'.

There was one other saint whose encounter with Maignenn is described in the 'Account'. This was Molasius of Leighlin, who was also known as Molaise or Laisren. Earlier in life Molasius had spent a period as a hermit on Holy Island, off Arran in Scotland. Later he had gone to Rome, where he stayed fourteen years as 'he felt a great desire to perfect himself in learning and science'. On his return to Ireland he became a famous bishop at Leighlin and took Rome's side in the major dispute with elements in the Irish church over the timing of Easter. The 'Account' describes how Maignenn called on Molasius of Leighlin at his 'house':

> now Molasius was so that in his body were thirty diseases, and he (for devotion's sake) penned in a narrow hovel. Moreover he was thus: spread out in form of a cross, with his mouth to the ground and he weeping vehemently, the earth under him being wet with his tears of penitence. Maignenn said: 'I adjure thee by God, and tell me wherefore thou askedst of Him that in thy body there must be three score and ten diseases'. Molasius answered: 'I will declare it, holy bishop: my condition is revealed to me as being such that my sinfulness like a flame pervades my body [his name means in English 'my brightness' or 'flame']; therefore, I am fain to have my purgatory here, and 'on the yonder side' to find the life eternal. Knowest thou, Maignenn, how the grain of wheat uses to be before it is sown in the earth [*sic*]: that it must needs be threshed and beaten? Even in like wise it is that, or [before] I be laid into the grave, I would have my body to be threshed by these infirmities; and to God be thanks for it that, how near soever death be to me now, thou art come my way before I die. For God's love, lay me out becomingly; perform thou the order of my sepulture and burial'.

Accordingly Maignenn carried out the order of these obsequies, which made the third most exalted burial that was done in Ireland: Patrick in *dún dá leth nglas* [Downpatrick]; Mochuda in Raithin of O Suanaig; and Molasius that by holy bishop Maignenn was buried.

Of such 'an exalted burial' there is no mention in O'Hanlon's account of Molasius. He says simply that the latter died about 638 and was buried in the church which he had founded. What remains of his monastery is a high cross by a holy well and the base of another cross. Like Maignenn's settlement at Kilmainham, that of Molasius at Leighlin has been obliterated.[15]

PROPHECY

Like many early Irish saints, Maignenn was given to prophesy. Some of it, as found in the 'Account' of his life, has quite a modern, if not eternal, ring to it:

> a time should come where there should be daughters flippant and tart, devoid of obedience to their mothers; when they of low estate should make much murmuring, and seniors lack reverent cherishing; where there should be impious laymen and prelates both, perverted wicked judges, disrespect to elders; soil barren of fruits, weather deranged and intemperate seasons; women given up to witchcraft, churches unfrequented, deceitful hearts and perfidy on the increase; a time when God's commandments should be violated and Doomsday's tokens occur every year.

Quite remarkable is the prophetic note on which the 'Account' ends, apparently unfinished. The prophecy is of a kind and content which was quite common in tales of the Irish saints which were circulating in the Middle Ages. In the course of it Maignenn refers to the 'Roth Rámach' or 'Rowing Wheel'. This was believed to be a sort of infernal machine which would herald the visitation of divine vengeance on the unrepentant. Together with the fiery dragon known as the 'broom out of Fanait' and the fatal day of fire of Saint John the Baptist, the 'Roth Rámach' is 'often mentioned [and] mysteriously spoken of in the old manuscripts'. It was said to be an artefact of Simon Magus, arch-opponent of the early apostles, who manufactured it in conjunction with the Irish druids and who intended it as a sign of his superiority over the apostles of Christ. The 'Roth Rámach', which has also been seen as a possible legacy of an earlier cult of sun-worship, was used as a symbol by the church for its own moral purposes.[16]

The mysterious fire of Kilmainham

The primal fire was kindled at Uisneach by the wizard Midhe and spread its blaze to the four ends of Ireland. Irish children have long been taught the story of that crucial moment at Easter when Patrick kindled his 'consecrated fire' for mass in defiance of the existing order.[1]

Fire too has a special significance in the 'Account' of Maignenn. Thus Maelruain of Tallaght honours the saint of Kilmainham by announcing that

> to thy successors' see great prerogatives shall belong, and in Ireland thy fire shall be the third on which privilege [of sanctity?] shall be conferred, i.e. the fire of the elder Lianan of Kinvarra, the lively and perennial fire that is in Inishmurray and Maignenn's fire in Kilmainham.

We have no other reference to this special fire at Kilmainham, but the fact that it is ranked with the fire of Inishmurray allows us to pursue the matter.

In the 1880s W.P.Wakeman visited the island of Inishmurray, which lies in the Atlantic Ocean almost five miles off the coast of Co. Sligo. He has left us a detailed description of the island, one which was recently corroborated by a local writer who was reared there. The last inhabitants left Inishmurray in 1948.[2]

In describing the ancient monuments of Inishmurray, and in particular the main enclosure known as 'the Cashel', Wakeman turns his attention to one particular building known as 'Teampall na Teine' or 'Teach na Teine', meaning respectively 'church of the fire' or 'house of the fire'. This was once used by the monks who lived on the island.

Wakeman writes angrily of how the Board of Public Works had lately botched the 'restoration' of the island's ruins, restructuring and erecting walls and entirely destroying the 'Leac-na-teinidh' or 'Stone of the fire' which for ages had covered a miraculous hearth in the 'house of the fire'. He explains:

> The natives all aver that here, of old, burnt a perpetual fire, from whence all the hearths on the island, which from any cause had become extinguished, were rekindled. Some say that it was only necessary to place a sod of turf upon the now missing Leac [stone], when miraculous combustion immediately ensued. Others declare that the sought-for fire was given out in the shape of a small burning

'coal' but all agree that from Leac-na-Teinidh, and from it alone all the island fires were kindled or relit.

A time, however, arrived, how long ago it is impossible to determine, when the famous hearth was to be ignominiously quenched for ever. The story of its extinction, universally told and believed by the islanders, is as follows: 'In the old time a stranger, said to have been a Scot, who had casually landed upon Inishmurray, on hearing of the wonderful hearth, at once proceeded to the Teach, where he found the fire, as usual, smouldering'.

It is not necessary here to detail exactly the further action of the visitor. Suffice it to say that, probably out of idle bravado, he shamefully desecrated the Leac, 'and lo! a miracle was the immediate result. The fire which up to that fatal moment had been scarcely visible at once flared up, and swiftly assumed the strength and appearance of a living fiery furnace, its flames leaping and enveloping the wretched victim, so that he could neither struggle against them nor fly, and stood melting, as it were, into nothingness, so that after a moment little remained but fragmentary bones, cracked and distorted'.

Flagstones are also found at the site of many holy wells and are regarded in folklore as having been left by Saint Patrick when he circumambulated the whole of Ireland. Their symbolic significance is associated with the transformation of these sites from pagan to Christian uses. Perhaps certain ancient fires were similarly blessed or 'privileged' by the early church.

In relation to that other fire of 'Lianan of Kinvarra' I have found nothing. However, one 'Liad(h)ain of Killyon', who flourished during the infancy of the Christian church in Ireland and who was the mother of Ciaran of Saigir, was the guardian of a 'hallowed fire'. Thus the Book of Lismore relates how a farmer from the monastic settlement of St Ciaran of Clonmacnoise went to visit Ciaran of Saigir [Seirkieran, Co. Offaly] and remained there a long time. Then, 'the Devil seduced him to quench the hallowed fire which the monks kept in the kitchen'. When he had done so, he left but was killed by wolves. Fortunately, he was brought back to life when Ciaran of Clonmacnoise arrived and invoked fire from heaven to rekindle the fire of Saigir. In this instance Ciaran of Clonmacnoise took down the fire from heaven onto his breast and transported it a distance without being hurt. Similarly, there are stories told of female saints who because of innocence could carry a burning ember in their skirts or aprons.[3]

It is not surprising to find a woman connected at this time with sacred fire, for it is well-known that St Brighid was reputed to have tended a remarkable blaze in Kildare. Attempts were made by outsiders to extinguish this fire too. Eight hundred years ago a visiting Anglo-Welsh cleric, Giraldus Cambrensis, described Brighid's fire thus:

At Kildare, famous for St Bridget are many miracles worthy to be
remembered, among which is St Bridget's fire, which they call inex-
tinguishable, not that it cannot be extinguished, but because the
nuns and holy women, by a continual supply of materials, have preserved it alive for so many years since the time of that virgin, and
tho[ugh] so great a quantity of wood has been consumed in it, yet
no ashes remain

Like the site in Inishmurray, that in Kildare was also surrounded by a
protective circle, although in the latter case it consisted of a hedge rather
than a stone wall.

Cambrensis says that across this
one day had come an archer,
who blew out the fire. He
immediately went mad and ran
about, approaching people and
blowing in their mouths as he
had blown in the fire. He was
brought to a stream where he
drank so much water that his
stomach burst. Another intruder
was dragged back by friends
when he had stretched only one
leg beyond the hedge, yet he too
went mad and was left permanently
lame in that limb.

2 The man who blew out Brighid's
holy fire (drawn before AD 1500).

Cambrensis writes that at Kildare the fire was tended by twenty women,
including Brighid. These must never blow the fire, but only use a bellows
or winnowing forks. After the saint's death the number never increased
beyond nineteen and one of these would tend the fire every night. On the
last night of each cycle, says Cambrensis, 'the nineteenth nun puts the logs
beside the fire and says "Brighid, guard your fire. This is your night". And
in this way the fire is left there, and in the morning the wood, as usual, has
been burnt and the fire is still lighting'.[4]

It was not simply mischief-makers who attempted to put out these sacred fires. Writing in the mid-seventeenth century, Ware tells us that the
fire of Kildare

> was put out by Henry Loundres, archbishop of Dublin, in the year
> 1220, says an anonymous author, of the order of predicants, who
> compendiously writ the annals of Ireland from the year of our Lord
> 1163, to 1314, wherein he lived.

However it were, the custom of preserving a fire in that nunnery of St Bridget (for the benefit of the poor and strangers) continued till the suppression of abbeys under Henry VIII.

Noting that this custom was 'not being used elsewhere' in Ireland in 1220, Ware speculates that the archbishop regarded it as imitating the practices of Rome's vestal virgins. It is, however, more logical to assume that the custom was of an indigenous Gaelic nature and the existence of the 'fire-house' on Innishmurray bolsters that assumption.[5]

There was a 'Teampall na mBan' or 'church of the women' on Innishmurray, but it is not known if on that island, as in Kildare, the sacred fire was kept going by women. The only evidence of females or nuns at Kilmainham appears to be an entry in the Book of Leinster which records 26 October as the feast day of 'Dairinill et Darbellinn et Comgell, Cill Magnenn', although another source gives 'cill n-ingen' or 'cell of the daughters' for 'Cill Maignenn'.[6]

The building which is now known as the 'fire-house' on Inishmurray is no older than the fourteenth century, according to Wakeman. Yet it is clear from the 'Account' of Maignenn, which was written not later than the fifteenth century, that the fire of Inishmurray had by then been long enough established to be thought of as having been famous in the days of Maignenn. Indeed Wakeman thinks that an earlier structure stood on the same site and there remains a 'souterrain' or under-ground passage close by the 'fire-house', which is clearly visible in a photograph reproduced by Heraughty. This indicates much earlier activity. The island is thought to have been inhabited at least one thousand years before Christ and Wakeman considers it unlikely that monks would have needed or constructed such a fortification as that which surrounds the Cashel on Inishmurray. This resembles pre-Christian structures elsewhere.

Wakeman's ire at the Board of Public Works and at their insensitive 'restoration' reaches a pitch when he considers their complete destruction of the 'Leach-na-Teinidh':

> It was, I believe, the only relic remaining in Ireland which appeared to be connected in some way, perhaps long forgotten, with the mysterious fire-worship practised by our Aryan forefathers.

SACRIFICE

If Kilmainham and the other places mentioned above were the locations of ancient sacred fires then it may be asked if these fires were once used for ceremonies which involved animal, or even human sacrifices. Bones shown to Wakeman on Inishmurray take on a sinister significance when viewed in such a light. These were located in a niche in the gable of the fire-house and were, he says, 'evidently human, and having apparently been under the action of intense-fire'.

A continuity of sacred usage has been established at other holy places, but this does not vitiate the fact that successive ages have consciously rejected as unacceptable particular practices of an earlier period. Thus, human sacrifice gave way to that of animals and this in turn was commuted to simpler ceremonies. Even before Christianity spread across Europe, the Romans were suppressing human sacrifices and the Christian Church too soon found itself attempting to usurp or to transform older beliefs.

A possible faint trace of earlier days may be discerned in one passage in the 'Account of Maignenn'. When the saint visited Maelruain of Tallaght he received a great welcome. Maelruain

> reached his hand across him and from the hem of the hair integument that he wore next his skin plucked a strong fibula with which he dealt himself a blow in the breast on the gospel side. Out of the pin's place issued not blood but merely a little pinkish fluid; and the motive of this ordeal was to announce to bishop Maignenn that in Maelruain's body pride existed not. Maignenn replied: 'I see that ...'

If there is here a distant echo of the way in which the druids divined the future from the physical reactions of their sacrificial victims, Maelruain's action may more simply be explained by reference to the fact that the rate at which blood spurted was regarded as a measure of one's lust or passion.[7]

The druids were not entirely given over to sacrifice. Other forms of divination and magic were less bloody. In the ninth-century glossary of Cormac we read that on Bealtaine the druids used to make two fires and that they used to drive the cattle through these as a safeguard against diseases. The similarities between such practices and later celebrations and customs, such as those surrounding the lighting of bonfires or 'bone-fires' on St John's Eve at Kilmainham and elsewhere, will become obvious when those customs are discussed in greater detail below.[8]

The Vikings and Brian Boru

The death of Maignenn, whenever it occurred in the seventh century, is likely to have been an occasion of much mourning for the inhabitants of his monastery at Kilmainham.

No contemporary description of the community survives but, if it was like many other Irish monasteries, Kilmainham originally comprised a circular enclosure, with wooden huts scattered around one or more cells or churches. Whether in wood or stone, such cells were not built to house great congregations, as may be seen today from the reconstruction of St Ciaran's cell at Clonmacnoise or from a visit to Glendalough. The new religious settlements stood out in an Irish landscape which then lacked towns or even villages. The members of those communities which formed in and around the monasteries were known collectively as 'manaig', an Irish term which included not only monks but also their tenant farmers and other lay people.[1]

The monks of Kilmainham lived on a high fertile ridge, suitable for grazing cattle. With fish being a staple of the Irish monastic diet, it is likely that they kept boats on the Liffey – in fine weather putting to sea and in bad staying on the river in pursuit of salmon.[2] The ford of Kylmehanok lay a little to the west of where Sarah Bridge now spans the Liffey and a weir in the same vicinity today marks, approximately, the point from which the river becomes tidal. Kylmehanok is said to have taken its name from a church or 'cell' which may have stood in the area of the present Phoenix Park, at a point half-way along a straight line between the Wellington Monument and the Magazine Fort.[3]

There is a single indication that, during the 'Golden Age' of the Irish church in the seventh and eight centuries, a 'school' of some kind developed at Kilmainham. Thus, in the 'Book of Lecan', there occurs an isolated reference to one 'Eochaid, of Cluain Rathach and magister of Kilmainham'. Certainly, at many Irish monasteries the monks and their pupils studied not only the bible but also classical Latin. Manuscripts were kept in leather satchels hanging on the walls and were used for instructional purposes.[4]

We get just one other glimpse of the inhabitants of the area before the arrival of the Vikings and the Anglo-Normans. More than a century after Maignenn's death, Lerghus Ua Fidhchain is said to have died at Kilmainham. This event, during the 780s, was noted by the old Irish annalists whose records have come down to us largely through later transcriptions. Lergus was renowned, ostensibly for his wisdom but possibly as a healer.[5]

VIKINGS

Into the lives of any such masters and sages, one day late in the first half of
the ninth century, sailed the Vikings. They had already ransacked Colum
Cille's island of Iona and spread terror along the north coasts of Britain and
Ireland. About the time of their appearance on the Liffey an author com-
posing a collection of the 'triads' of Ireland described Kilmainham as being
one of 'the three places of Ireland to alight at'. The other two were Derry
and Taghmon, where stood the old monasteries of Colum Cille and Munnu
respectively. From this reference it seems that the three institutions had
acquired a reputation for hospitality and were desirable destinations for those
arriving from Scotland, England and Wales.[6]

It is thought likely by a number of contemporary scholars that the Vikings sailed right up the River Liffey and captured Kilmainham, which
stood in a strategically important position above the river mouth and the
ford of Áth-Cliath. Such an attack would have been consistent with their
seizure of other monasteries on both sides of the Irish Sea. Soon they had
brought women from Scandinavia to join them and were fishing for salmon
in the Liffey. A Norse fort has been found as far west as Clondalkin. The
sites of two substantial cemeteries, one at Islandbridge and the other at
Kilmainham, have yielded many valuable finds and establish the area as
possibly the most important Viking burial ground outside of Scandinavia.
Clarke remarks that 'it will not come as a surprise if the *longphort* turns up in
the Islandbridge-Kilmainham area'. The elusive *longphort* was the place where
the trading and piratical Vikings kept their boats, archaeological remains of
which have yet to be located.[7]

The Céli Dé communities at Tallaght and Finglas are said to have been
more fortunate than other monastic communities. They were apparently
spared the excesses visited by the Vikings on monasteries further afield,
perhaps because of their poverty.[8]

There is no doubt that the Vikings had a cemetery at Kilmainham and,
although no remains of it have been identified, a cemetery is also likely to
have been part of Maignenn's enclosure. Such was the case at other monasteries in Ireland and the most likely site of such a cemetery at Kilmainham is
in the vicinity of the graveyard known as 'Bully's Acre', of which more
below. Smyth allows that the land to the east of this, including that area
where the Royal Hospital would later rise, possibly became a Viking 'green'
similar to that outside the eastern wall of the new city of Dublin. If it was
such a 'green', then one may reasonably ask if it too was marked by a
Viking 'thing' or standing stone. It must be admitted that the possibility of
it being a Viking 'green' rests on an ambiguity in the 'Cogadh Gaedhel re
Gallaibh'.[9]

Given their extensive seafaring needs, the Vikings had an incentive to construct houses and other buildings at the river mouth to the east of Kilmainham. In the ninth century they began to develop their new city of Dublin, where before there seems to have been little more than a river-crossing. The fact that 'the cross' of Kilmainham was to be defined as the western extremity of the 'ridings' of Dublin when the Normans arrived suggests that it was earlier a place to meet those approaching from Leinster and Meath, as well as from the west of Ireland. Like the Golan Heights between Israel and Syria today, Kilmainham straddled an important frontier.[10]

BRIAN BORU

Its strategic position meant that Kilmainham witnessed the clashes of various armies. Thus, for example, on 15 September 919 at the ford of Kylmehanok, Niall Glúndubh, or 'Black-knee', led a combined force of Irish against Dublin. He was mortally wounded and his army routed by the Danes. That force was more representative of the country as a whole than was the famous and successful army assembled almost a century later by Brian Boru. In 1013, the year before Brian defeated the Scandinavians and their Irish allies at the battle of Clontarf, he or his son Murchadh plundered much of Leinster,

> and he devastated the whole country, until he reached the community of Caimhghen [Kevin, Glendalough], and he ravaged and burnt the whole country; and many captives were carried off by him, and cattle innumerable; and he came to Cill-Maighnenn to the Green of Áth Cliath ...

The author of this account, writing no later than the twelfth century, goes on to state that Brian and Murchadh and the army joined up at Kilmainham and 'made a siege and a blockade around Áth Cliath, and an encampment there'. The siege dragged on until Christmas. Then with provisions running out, Brian and his forces went home.[11]

The record is phrased in such a way that it is not clear whether Brian's soldiers stopped at Glendalough and Kilmainham or looted these communities along with the rest of Leinster. This would not have been surprising. At Clonmacnoise today an audio-visual presentation reminds visitors that, while it was a Tudor king who finally suppressed the religious orders, the monastery of St Ciaran had previously been sacked more often by native Irish forces than by the Vikings and English put together.

Whatever ambiguity surrounds the actions of Brian's force at Kilmainham in 1013, there is none in an account of what happened the following year.

Although the information has generally been missed or ignored as unpalatable by historians, an old chronicle tells us in plain and simple language that on the eve of the Battle of Clontarf:

> Brian burnt Kilmainham.[12]

Brian's army was then massing about the city and lighting many fires in order to terrify its inhabitants. It was the week before Easter and these blazes had a symbolic resonance for Irish Christians, given Patrick's actions at Tara in particular. We know that the terrible prophecy of the 'Roth Rámach' had been used to frighten the Danes and that they took it seriously. In popular folklore the lighting of bonfires at midsummer continued for centuries to be associated with the demise of the Vikings.[13]

Perhaps Brian himself ought to have heeded another prophecy, namely the reported warning of Maignenn that those who persecuted his precinct would have a short and transient life and that their fruit would wither. For on Good Friday 1014, although their army triumphed, Brian and his son Murchadh died in battle while Kilmainham still smouldered. The following day his other son Donnchadh met with his colleagues at Kilmainham and slaughtered oxen on the Green of Áth Cliath.[14]

THE GRANITE SHAFT

Various annalists make it clear that the remains of Brian and Murchadh were taken north and buried at Armagh.[15] Nevertheless, there grew up later in Dublin a popular belief that one of them was buried at Kilmainham and that a high cross had been raised over his grave. This legend has given rise to one explanation for the origin of the decorated shaft which still stands today, sadly neglected on the site of Maignenn's monastery.[16] In fact there is no evidence that a cross was raised to commemorate those slain in battle, or even to thank God for victory, and none that monks were found at Kilmainham in the period after Clontarf. It cannot even be taken for granted that the shaft once served as the upright of a cross. It may have been a standing stone or Viking marker which survived from an earlier period and was later decorated in Gaelic or Hiberno-Norse style.

The spiral decoration on the east face bears some similarity to that on some 'very early' monastic slabs, a number of which were 'christianised' by the addition of symbols to existing monuments. The surviving examples of such slabs are generally smaller and are less rectangular than the stone at Kilmainham, which is three metres high. Crawford has described the Kilmainham shaft as 'massive'. It is granite.[17] Visible close up at the top of the east face is some ribbing, which is ostensibly in the shape of a large 'm' but possibly a continuation of some design on a top stone which has since gone missing.

There is some evidence which lends weight to a hypothesis that, before or after the Battle of Clontarf, an existing monument was decorated or adapted, perhaps to make a cross.

Firstly, as indicated earlier, this whole area was an important Viking graveyard. Secondly, it is said that a number of coins and a fine sword, all ostensibly Viking, were in the late eighteenth century found at the base of the shaft and this may suggest that here was an important Viking grave. As against that, however, the shaft had previously been taken down and it is possible that it was not re-erected in the same spot. We

3 Granite shaft (east face) at Bully's Acre.

do not know if the large flat stone in which it stands was also moved.

Thirdly, Harbison thinks that the shaft is most probably ninth to eleventh century and he notes that the tops of the sides have been partly cut away, 'leaving the top of the cross in the form of a tenon, suggesting the possibility of the use of carpentry techniques in attaching the arms, which are now missing'. This information is consistent with arms having been added to an existing stone, which was decorated in situ with those simple and unusual designs which will be discussed again below. However, it is equally consistent with there having been from the date of its erection a further stone, perhaps cruciform, perhaps not, on top of the shaft.[18]

Monastic manuscripts from Kilmainham might help to solve the puzzle of the decoration on the shaft but none has been found or identified. Imaginative speculation about the origins of the unusual shaft remains just that.

There is, as we have seen, evidence that a monastery functioned at Kilmainham in the seventh and eight centuries but there is none that it survived the ninth. Of Kilmainham's fate after the Battle of Clontarf, outside the walls of the Hiberno-Norse town of Dublin, no record has been discovered. The only hints of a late survival of the monastic community are the granite shaft and a bell, ostensibly from the same period, which has been found buried at Kilmainham and which is shown below. This bell, writes Bourke, is unusually deep in relation to its height and its depth diminishes very gradually towards the crown. The bulging form of the bell is without parallel [in its class]. On both terminals of the handle there is a knob which faces towards the side from above the shoulder of the bell. Both preserve the proportion of human heads and that they were intended as such is not to be doubted when they are viewed in profile.

4a Medieval bell found at Kilmainham, now in the National Museum.

4b Detail of above bell, showing worn heads.

This distinctive bell, which is now preserved at the National Museum in Dublin, appears to be that which was reported in the nineteenth century to have been discovered during the work on the new railway line at Kilmainham.[19]

Norman Knights

In 1170 another army assembled outside Dublin. Stretching from the cairn at what is now Dolphin's Barn, the forces of Dermot MacMurrough and his Welsh and Anglo-Norman allies entrenched themselves in anticipation of their capture of Dublin.[1]

Soon not only the city but much of Ireland was under the sway of the Normans and the native monks were powerless to prevent new religious orders from arriving and taking possession of their old lands. Prominent amongst the newcomers were the Knights of Saint John of Jerusalem, whose order had been founded in the wake of the crusades. They constituted a military and religious organisation whose members took vows and were expected to be devoted especially to prayer and to good works. The English division of the order was granted extensive properties in Ireland, where it established many 'preceptories' or houses. Ware explains that an establishment at Kilmainham was

> Founded for Knights of the Order of St John Baptist of Jerusalem, commonly called Knights Hospitallers, by Richard, Sir-named Strongbow, earl of Pembroke, or Strigul, about the year 1174. And Hen. II confirmed the endowments. It was afterwards mightily enrich'd by the donations of others, and especially under Edw. II when the revenue of the Templars then newly suppres'd were granted to this order, Walter del Ewe being then prior of the Hospitallers. This priory was likewise an hospital for strangers and pilgrims.[2]

All modern authorities agree with Ware that Kilmainham was granted by Strongbow to the Knights Hospitallers. Indeed the first prior is said to have been 'probably a brother' of Strongbow's marshal. Authorities now dismiss earlier suggestions that Kilmainham once belonged to the Knights Templar. This error appears to have been made first by L.A. Alemand and copied from him by Archdall and others, through whom the idea passed into later accounts. Archdall actually cites Ware as his source but, as may be seen above, Ware states clearly that the site at Kilmainham was given to the Hospitallers and later enriched from Templar property when the Templars were suppressed. The thought of Templars at Kilmainham has a romantic appeal to some and the *Irish Times* carried 'a long and animated correspondence' when Falkiner publicly rebutted the idea in 1907.[3]

The knights were given by Hugh Tyrel of Castleknock a grant of about 500 acres, later mostly comprised in the Phoenix Park. As they came to dominate the high ground on both sides of the river west of Dublin, they were soon embroiled in a disagreement with its citizens respecting new mills and a pool ('*stagnum*') which the knights created on the Liffey. In 1223 they were ordered to place these 'in the same state as they were at the departure from that city of King John [1210]'. This indicates the existence of an older mill, one dating from before the Anglo-Norman invasion or erected by the knights after their arrival at Kilmainham. There was also a weir at Kilmainham, and others at Chapelizod, Palmerstown and Lucan. At these, it was reported in 1306, 'the course of the water was accustomed to be of the breadth of sixteenth feet at least, with sufficient depth for the passage of boats, bundles of firewood and fish'.[4]

In the ancient records of the city of Dublin and in other sources, 'the privileges and liberties' of the city were defined after 1200 as extending 'to the bounds of the land of Kilmeinan [Kilmainham], and thence beyond the water of Kilmeinan, near the Avenclith [Liffey] to the forde of Kilmehafoch'.

5 Knight Hospitaller of St John. Artist unknown.

Citizens who annually rode these boundaries passed under the middle arch of Bow Bridge, down through the fields, by 'the cross' of Kilmainham, and over the Liffey. But it is unclear whether or not this 'cross' was a religious monument or a cross-roads.[5]

There survives from 1305 a solitary glimpse of life for the ordinary people of Kilmainham in the early fourteenth century. From it we find that they were very much put upon by a man called Benedict, who ended up being charged with robbery in the following circumstances.

Out in the meadows one Peter was mowing when, for reasons we are not told, the local sergeant arrived and carried away Peter's sickle 'through the town of Kilmainham'. Peter came complaining to Benedict, Thomas and Robert that he could not do his work, so they followed the sergeant and attacked him:

> And Benedict was about to strike him on the head with an axe which he carried, but was prevented by a woman who ran between them. On account of which Benedict threw her to the ground.

They proceeded to beat the sergeant and took the sickle from him. Benedict and his friends having been subsequently charged, the court heard that Benedict was notorious locally:

> [He] was accustomed by stealth to carry bread, ale and other victuals, from the manor of Kilmainham by night, and to enter the town there, and break doors of houses, and beat those whom he found, against whom he might be angry, and to take them and put them in the stocks, to wit [for example], William, son of Thomas, against whom he was very angry because William imputed to him [that he took] the goods of the house of Kilmainham.

On a legal technicality, Benedict and his friends were fortunate to be found guilty not of robbery but of deforcement done against the peace. They were committed to gaol.

Even more fortunate, six years later, were a couple of sailors who had forcibly assisted in the killing of one Robert Thurstayn, whose name suggests that he was of Scandinavian descent. The couple, Robert Godard of Sandewiz and Richard, son of Robert Faber of Liverpool, were sentenced to death by hanging:

> Afterwards Robert Godard and Richard were taken down as dead from the gallows, and when carried in a cart to Kilmainham to be buried were found to be alive and took refuge in a church there, and at the instance of John de Ergadia, who asserts that they had set out

with him to pay homage to the King in Scotland, and testifies that
they are valiant and good mariners, suit of the peace is pardoned to
them.[6]

During the two centuries following the Anglo-Norman invasion of Ireland the properties and persons of the Knights Hospitallers played an important role in support of the occupation. Many leading members of the
government, including lords deputies, were members of the order. Lying
just beyond the city of Dublin's jurisdiction, Kilmainham was the official
residence of the Grand Prior of Ireland, with his staff of knights, squires,
chaplains, clerks and inferior attendants in great number and variety, including craftsmen, servants and labourers.[7]

Some records of Kilmainham priory have survived and a number of
articles have been published dealing with aspects of this period at Kilmainham.
If Maignenn's foundation perhaps once stood on the location of the old
graveyard, which is now closed, the priory of St John appears to have stretched
around it. The newcomers arrived with their own intellectual apparatus,
one which was both militaristic and cultural. Throughout its time in Ireland
the order is said to have 'retained an alien spirit'. The knights of the priory
had few if any Irish sympathies and were ready to turn their arms against
their Irish neighbours.[8]

While it is not intended to repeat once more what is known of the
Hospitallers in Dublin, part of Charles McNeill's description of 1922 is
worth giving here:

> The House of Kilmainham, therefore, covered a considerable area. It
> comprised an inner and an outer enclosure. The inner enclosure was
> the Castle, a quadrangle surrounded by a strong wall with towers at
> the four corners and an outer ditch. The principal gate was under a
> tower on the eastern side, and there was also a postern near one of
> the corner towers apparently towards the north. Within the quad-
> rangle were a number of detached buildings: the residence of the
> prior; two dormitories for the brethren, some of whom seem to have
> had their own *camerae* or apartments, and the preceptor had his *cam-
> era* among them; lodgings for a number of the permanent guests,
> allotted in the towers on the walls or in other buildings; an internal
> chapel; and a prison, '*tetra domus de Malrepos*', the dismal house of
> Little-ease.
>
> The most striking building within the castle was the great hall, a
> splendid apartment in which all the residents of the house, unless
> disabled, met to take their meals. For each class there was a special
> table ...

The outer enclosure surrounded the castle on every side, and formed what was known as the manor-close, mansion or Court of Kilmainham. Its main gate was on the southern side facing the Common Green of Kilmainham, [and was] a commanding structure with dwelling rooms in its upper stories which at a much later date were assigned to be the residence of the person appointed to be the Queen's Keeper of the House at Kilmainham.

Within this gate were orchards, shrubberies and gardens, amidst which stood many buildings of various kinds, such as the *camerae* or separate dwellings of permanent guests, farm-buildings, hay-barns, granaries, stables ... forges, a carpenter's shop, a brew-house, a dairy, etc.

The church of St John of Kilmainham, which was parochial as well as conventual, stood near the ancient cross in the cemetery considerably to the east of the buildings already described.[9]

McNeill was able to abstract a picture of life at Kilmainham between 1326 and 1339 from that 'beautifully-written' register of the priory which has survived and which is kept at Oxford in the Bodleian Library. This has been published in Latin by the Irish Manuscript Commission, with a substantial introduction in English by McNeill, but there is also an earlier English translation at the Royal Irish Academy. Many of the entries in the register refer to leases at Kilmainham and at other properties belonging to the knights and we learn from it that in addition to the expected rents there would often be demanded an annual token such as capons (fattened cock fowls) or, in one case, 'the service of a rose'. One man was treated favourably 'on account of the devout love which we have found in the same William towards St John the Baptist, our patron'. The feast of the nativity of St John (24 June) was one of a number of days which regularly occur as reference points in leases, the others being Easter and Christmas and the feasts of the Blessed Virgin Mary in March and September. The register also contains much information on the conditions of occupancy for those who wished to live at Kilmainham, covering matters such as meat and drink and the position of servants, as well as hay, corn, horse-litter, candles, wax and horse-shoeing. The drink of the house was beer, with the knights having their own brew-house. The absence of references to wine, which was widely available in Ireland, the expectation that residents dine in common and mentions of regular fasts are reminders that the priory was a religious institution as well as a place for the powerful to meet. When the prior got special permission to have food brought to his chamber in order to confer 'secretly' with friends of the order, it was recorded in the register.[10]

The term 'hospital' was used then to apply not only to institutions for the ailing but also to big town houses and even to inns of court. The 'Hospital of Saint John of Jerusalem' at Kilmainham operated as a guest-house and 'private nursing-home' rather than as an infirmary or almshouse. In this respect and others it should be distinguished from the 'Hospital of St John' which stood not far away by Dublin's Newgate. At Kilmainham the more that one contributed materially as a guest of the knights, the better were the service and accommodation provided. The Knights Hospitallers erected many buildings and made improvements to the area, although it is not known if it was they who erected the bridge of six arches which was in the sixteenth century described as 'having been built in ancient times'. This straddled the little islands which lay in the river at the ford of Kylmehanok, thus giving rise to the name of 'Islandbridge'. It was one of the charitable functions of medieval religious orders to make and to maintain bridges for travellers. In any event, the bridge connected the knights' lands on both sides of the Liffey. There was also, at the manor-close, a turning or draw-bridge of some kind, perhaps across the Camac.[11]

The knights also took some responsibility for the poor and, in particular, for the care of lepers. Perhaps they inherited this duty along with the property of Kilmainham, for we saw above that an old leper woman is said to have supplied milk to the 'the poor, the needy and the palsied' in Maignenn's time. The knights endowed a leper-house at the most western limits of their lands, at Chapelizod, and appointed a warden to manage it. The leper-house was under the patronage of St Laurence the martyr. In 1336 one 'John' was granted 'the care and custody of the house of the sick of the B[lessed] Laurence near Dublin', on the specific grounds that he had previously demonstrated towards it 'very cordial affection and devoted love'. It is said to have been closed in 1426, when its owner surrendered custody of it and of its lands to the crown. Yet, still in 1699, one of the earliest entries in the records of the new Royal Hospital refers to 'the lazors and lepers and the lands belonging to them'.[12]

Not only did the knights help to consolidate the Anglo-Norman presence in Ireland but they aided the English king in France. In 1418 Prior Bottiller and a great number of Irish came out of Ireland, 'in mail, with darts and skeyns', to assist Henry V at the siege of Rouen. However, their days of glory were drawing to a close and by the end of the fifteenth century the prior was an 'unruly' man of ill-repute and the institution was in decline. In the first half of the sixteenth century stability was restored under Prior Rawson, although in keeping with the times he felt free to benefit himself and his family from the lands of the order. The property of the priory had once stretched nearly two miles along the south bank of the Liffey but much of it had been alienated before the knights, along with all religious orders, were suppressed by King Henry VIII. In 1541 Rawson surrendered the remaining property of the Hospitallers. Bradshaw notes that Kilmainham was the last Irish establishment to be dissolved.[13]

Although it was said that Rawson 'kept the best house' in Dublin after the Lord Deputy, his castle was in poor repair. This was remarked upon by officials who prepared an 'extent' of the place on behalf of the state:

> The house, mansions and buildings on the site of the manor, which was the principal hospice of the prior and brethren, are very necessary and very well suited to be a mansion and habitation for the king's Deputy in Ireland. They are at present in great decay.

The 'extent' of 1541 also discloses that the knights had kept a 'water mill operating on the River Amblyffe [Liffey] with two pairs of mill-stones under the same roof' and, as we already know, 'a weir on the same river for catching salmon'. There was also, 'on the south of the house a fulling-mill between the house and stream called the Cammocke'. 'Fulling' is the process of cleansing and thickening cloth by washing and beating. Cloth mills would continue to be a feature of the area until the present day.[14]

The same officials provide a description of one of the knights' places of worship. McNeill suggests, as we saw above, that the priory church stood near the granite shaft which survives in the cemetery and 'to the east' of the other buildings described by him. It is recorded in the extent of 1541 that,

> The church annexed to the site is the parish church, and is at present too large. Part of it, namely the chapel on the south, can be thrown down without loss, and this ought to be done, as the parishioners owing to their extreme poverty are unable to maintain the church, and what would remain is sufficient for them.

Nearby lived James Whyte, an organist ('*organorum modulator*'), who was given a dwelling as tenant for life, as well as an annuity of 53s. 4d. and food and drink, 'provided he gave his services in the choir of the church at Kilmainham at certain times specified'.[15]

McNeill has also said that the churches connected with the houses of the Hospitallers in Ireland were not, as were those of most religious orders, the most important part of the establishment. He adds that they were primarily parochial. The priory, however, was exempt from the jurisdiction of the local bishop. In the 1330s, as we learn from the *Registrum*, there were ten chaplains perpetually appointed in the conventual church of St John, one of these being assigned to William Le Mareschal 'to celebrate for him the canonical hours and divine service in chapel in his oratory built by him for himself' in his chambers. There were at least two chapels associated with the institution. One of these, as we shall see in the next chapter, was known as 'St Mary's Chapel'. In the priory church itself there was appointed a special commemoration night for the soul of one man who had been of particular service to the knights. According to one account there was painted in many of the glass windows of Kilmainham priory the image of a hand and sleeved wrist, descending from a cloud and holding an anchor with a ring-head. The anchor was an early Christian symbol, common in mainland Europe and especially at Rome. A number of examples are found in Ireland. Beneath the anchor at Kilmainham was the word 'Athema'. The secondary source of this information assumes that by 'athema' was meant 'anathema' but this seems rash. The word 'athema' is not English or Latin and the closest Greek is 'hey themis' (η θεμις) meaning 'what is right' or 'what is decreed'. The same source says that the priory was demolished in 1612.[16]

There is now no trace of the priory church. In 1788 Walker referred to the existence then of a 'tiled floor' which may have marked its site but he did not give its location. In 1859 fragments of flooring tiles were said to have been 'dug up from under the portion of an ancient cross at the cemetery' and 'originally, no doubt,' formed a portion of one of the knights' churches. These were exhibited at the Royal Society of Antiquaries in Ireland. The shaft or 'ancient cross' stood in 1859 where it stands now, so if this report is correct then it suggests that one of the churches rose at Bully's Acre. As we shall see in the following chapter a map drawn in the seventeenth century as part of the Down survey also indicates the site of a church. In the epilogue, we shall suggest that these finds and others, along with the map, indicate that further archaeological investigation of the area is desirable.[17]

From princely castle to royal hospital

Kilmainham was the richest of the dissolved religious houses in the Pale. As noted above, the order had provided chief governors and many leading officials for the administration of Ireland and it is not surprising to find that the deputy and council now used the surrendered premises as a location for their meetings. Their enjoyment of it for such purposes was interrupted in the 1550s, when the priory of Kilmainham became the only institution to be restored to its pervious owners. This was during that brief period in the reign of Mary when it looked as though the Reformation might be stalled and the fortunes of Roman Catholics revived. Sir Oswald Messingberde was then appointed prior at Kilmainham.[1]

The recovery was short lived and Messingberde departed, a special statute being passed to convey the castle back into government hands. It was once again used for official business. There were some who considered the whole premises to be too unwieldy for conversion, with one writer in 1559 describing it as 'too ample a house for this world ... meter for a prince than for a deputy'. Criminals and women of ill repute appear to have been frequenting the range of buildings.[2]

According to Falkiner, in 1572 the author of a report on the 'decay of the manor-place of Kilmainham' noted that 'St John's Church' was roofless and that 'St Mary's Chapel' was being utilised as a stable, its steeple being broken. This may have been the chapel which was part of the parish church and which officials in 1541 had recommended be thrown down. It is unknown if repairs were undertaken on foot of the report of 1572 but the government continued to make use of the old priory or castle. In 1575 its vulnerability as an outpost of Dublin was exposed by a rumour that Kildare had devised that Rory Oge with 500 kerne (foot-soldiers) should go suddenly to Kilmainham and fetch away the lord deputy's wife and children, presumably as hostages. Shortly afterwards the continuing strategic importance of Kilmainham, straddling the western approaches to Dublin, was underlined when Lord Deputy Sidney had a new stone bridge erected across the river at Islandbridge, with insignia on it. This replaced the former one 'built in ancient times, with six arches, now very ruinous and dilapidated'. Sidney boasted of dining one afternoon under his cloth of estate in the great hall at Kilmainham and, two days later, displaying his pennant against O'Neill in the heart of Tyrone. During the reign of Elizabeth, certain customs called 'the Mary-gallons' were yearly levied from the inhabitants of the town of Kilmainham. These became known popularly as 'the merry gallons'.[3]

Once it had been repaired the castle at Kilmainham provided alternative
and airy accommodation for the head of the Irish administration during
warm summer months. An entry in the accounts of William Fitzwilliam,
lord deputy between 1588 and 1594, shows that the move from one venue
to the other involved the transport of large quantities of furniture and other
articles. It appears that the preferred mode of removal was not along the
narrow and dirty city streets but by the river. Provision is made for 'loads of
hangings and stuff from Kilmainham to Dublin by water and from the quay
to the castle [Dublin Castle]'.[4]

Kilmainham was soon abandoned again when political events took a
turn for the worse. Like so many Dublin buildings at the end of the sixteenth century, it was neglected while the Tudor conquest of Gaelic Ireland
continued and in 1604 it was reported:

> The abbey of Kilmainham is most ruinous, and yet the repairing
> thereof very chargeable to his majesty – and for the house no deputy
> hath used it since Sir William Fitzwilliam's time, but only as a garner
> to serve their grain, which may be laid up in the king's storehouse at
> Dublin far more commodiously.[5]

Most of the priory by this stage was roofless and there were fears that,
unless repaired, it 'will all fall to the ground'. It looked like it might win a
reprieve when Lord Deputy Chichester decided to repair the castle as a
place for himself in which to live and to work during the summer months,
as Dublin Castle 'is somewhat noisome [offensive/smelly] by reason of the
prison, and especially when it pleaseth God to visit the city of Dublin with
sickness, as of late years it hath been very grievously'.[6]

It is said, as we have seen, that in 1612 the priory church was demolished. Not long afterwards the house of the Phoenix was made an alternative residence for the lords deputies and the fortunes of the manor of
Kilmainham declined further. The Phoenix stood on the site of the present
magazine fort, to the north of Islandbridge, and it has been said to have
taken its name from the Irish words 'fionn uisce'. These, writes Falkiner,
denote clear or spring water. It is not known to what spring they might
refer and Ball suspects that the name 'Phoenix' may have been given to the
house simply because of the way in which it rose so magnificently on its
prominent site. Yet, if the lord deputies now favoured the north bank of the
river for their summer sojourns, Kilmainham itself continued to be used as
a location for the administration of justice and in 1626 an official 'inquisi-
tion' into certain matters relating to the titles of lands was held there.[7]

When decades of frustration erupted and the Gaelic and 'Old English'
communities of Ireland rose together in a major rebellion against the King,
Kilmainham was secured by the government and became one of the places

where outlawry proceedings were held to identify those guilty of treason. Among the men and women proclaimed outlaws was Dennis Connor of Kilmainham, described as 'meere' (mayor of Kilmainham?) and 'gent'.[8]

In 1655-6 Robert Girdler visited Kilmainham in order to survey the old parish. A map which he made has fortunately survived and is partly reproduced here. It shows that the parish included 'The Phoenix' and 'Newtowne' on the north side of the river, as well as Kilmainham, Inchicore and Dolphin's Barn on the south. He shows the remains of the knight's old priory and the village or town of Kilmainham. Girdler described the quality of land in the parish as 'arable meadow and pasture' and continued:

> On Kilmainham there stands the ruins of a large castle; a street of good habitable houses; two double mills and a single mill in repair; and an arched stone bridge across the River Liffey: at Inchicore the ruins of a brick house: at Dolphin's Barn two very fair houses; a mill

6 Down survey of Kilmainham and Islandbridge, showing ruins of the priory (by Girdler).

in repair and five thatched houses. At the Phoenix a very stately
house now in good repair.[9]

Girdler shows also a building marked by a cross, standing at the north-
eastern corner of the ruins. The priory's own church is said to have been
destroyed in 1612, as seen above, so the cross may mark merely its site or
that of one of the chapels. It was reported in 1859, as we saw earlier, that
Norman flooring tiles were dug up near the granite shaft in Bully's Acre and
that originally, 'no doubt', this was the site of one of the knights' churches.
McNeill himself, who is a careful researcher, also appears to have believed
that priory church was located near the granite shaft or 'ancient cross'.
However, for this to be the place marked by the cross in Girdler's map it
would be necessary for the inner enclosure of the knights which he shows
to have risen approximately opposite the present Kilmainham Gaol Museum, or even further west, and to have stretched east across the present
South Circular Road. The likelihood that this was so would be greater if it
could be shown that the old road down from Kilmainham highway to the
ford of Kylmehanok (itself up-river from the present bridge), must have lain
further west than the modern thoroughfare. Rocque's map of 1756 (see p.
50) provides evidence for this. On it the road is shown describing an arc in
a north-easterly direction from the highway, until it reaches a point at about
the site of the old St John's Well. Remarkably, the tree-lined avenue or
'elm walk' from the Royal Hospital, which was to be its first entrance, is
shown to stop some distance from this road, approximately at its present
terminus. That the arc enclosed a piece of the knights' land is likely, for it is
known that between the time of its establishment and the end of the eighteenth century the Royal Hospital lost control of some property in this area.
The avenue ended where it did because the public coming out from Dublin
over Bow Bridge had access from the highway to Bully's Acre and St John's
Well, on that line along which the South Circular Road was to be laid.[10]

During the mid-seventeenth century the old graveyard was still in use,
with at least one burial known to have taken place in the1650s. During that
decade of Cromwellian mayhem the population of Kilmainham is said to
have risen by 64%, an increase which reflected the influx to Dublin from
more troubled areas of Ireland. At this time 'the island mills' at Islandbridge
were supplying the army with all of its corn. Shortly before the restoration
of monarchy in 1660 a census found 130 people living at Kilmainham, of
whom seventy were described as 'Irish' and sixty as 'English'.[11]

After two decades of rebellion and Cromwellian activity, Ireland was at
last at peace in the 1660s. It was a period of growth for Dublin, a city which
now enjoyed the attentions of the duke of Ormond, who had been appointed lord lieutenant. It was he who conceived of a great deer-park on
lands in and around the house of the Phoenix, to the north of Islandbridge.

At first this park included most of the land which had belonged to the
Knights Hospitallers on the south side of the Liffey. Still at the time meadows ran down to the muddy river bank between James's Street and Islandbridge. The lands required for the Phoenix Park were enclosed by a stone
wall which met the water on each side at a point just west of the covered
portion of the modern Heuston station. The walls on the south bank of the

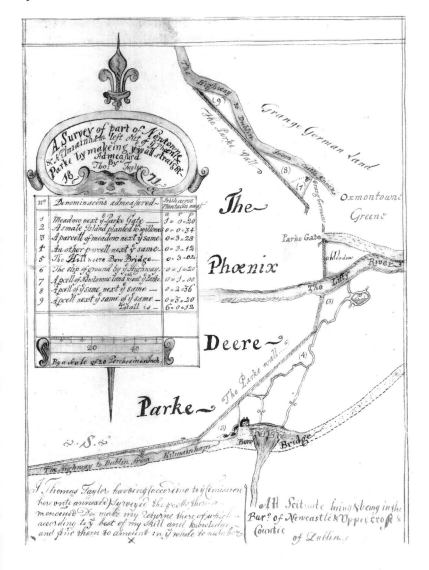

7 Walls of the Phoenix Park enclosing part of Kilmainham, by Thomas Taylor, 1671.

Liffey embraced the whole space which would later be comprised in the grounds of the Royal Hospital. Portion of this wall is shown in the fine survey of 1671 by Thomas Taylor, reproduced above. This includes a sketch of Bow Bridge which shows the arches under which the representatives of Dublin used to ride annually when marking out the bounds of their city.[12]

Within a few years, however, the decision to include portion of Kilmainham in the Phoenix Park was reversed when Ormond resolved to build at Kilmainham an institution for old and maimed soldiers. Most of the land which had belonged to the knights at the time of their surrender, stretching up from the south bank of the Liffey onto the brow of the ridge, was then designated by the government for this purpose. In all, the new Royal Hospital was granted sixty-four acres, with a further seven acres in the vicinity of Islandbridge being hived off the knights' old property for the solicitor-general, Sir John Temple. He in turn assigned these to William Robinson, who was the architect of the Royal Hospital, and the settlement around Islandbridge was soon the scene of a considerable amount of development. This may be seen from comparing a view painted by Bate about 1695 with a sketch by Place of 1698. Prominent in both is Davies' brewery, which stood near where a barracks would late rise. The district was also re-nowed for market gardens and a nursery where, reputedly, pineapples were first introduced into Ireland. These could be acquired locally under the sign of 'The Black Lion'. Islandbridge was also a place to buy fine flowers.[13]

Robinson's design for the new hospital is generally thought to have been inspired by that of *Les Invalides*, another institution for old soldiers

8 Francis Place, Dublin from the Phoenix Park, 1698. Detail showing Islandbridge.
This old bridge was further east than that erected in 1791.

which Louis XIV had erected in Paris. A similar royal hospital was soon to be opened at Chelsea in London. When the construction of that at Kilmainham commenced, the ruins of the buildings to the east were regarded as being merely a source of stone. In 1681 the letters patent which were issued by Charles II in connection with the establishment of the Royal Hospital noted that the new structure was to be erected 'near the old ruinous building commonly called the Castle of Kilmainham'. Colley writes:

> on the west part of the said ground had been formerly a large pile of buildings, which consisted of several quadrangles, but now all ruined, and most of the foundations dug up; there only remained standing in the year 1680 part of the walls of the chapel, the stones whereof were taken down and carefully removed to the new hospital, and wholly used in building the present chapel of the same'.[14]

Photographs taken in 1979 during restoration work at the Royal Hospital show stripped stone walls and cut blocks of sandstone. Sandstone, 'so common to the Norman structures ... was used until a later period in the buildings on the east coast'.[15]

Given that the knights had inherited an older monastic site, perhaps incorporating some of its walls in their own buildings, it is tempting to speculate that stones from the original cell of Maignenn may today form part of the present structure of the restored Royal Hospital or that the blocks which were photographed in 1979 were amongst those which the knights used to build their new priory when they came to Kilmainham. It has also

9 Sandstone blocks, exposed at the Royal Hospital during restoration and possibly from the priory of the knights.

been suggested that tracery in portion of a new window was re-used from an earlier building and, more particularly still, that the glass used in the upper part was medieval. Craig considered this unlikely.[16]

In 1698 John Dunton visited Kilmainham and later wrote in relation to the old priory that there were 'no marks of the convent of priors now to be seen'. Childers and Stewart, as we shall find below, discerned traces of foundations of the old institution in 1921 but it is clear from this reference by Dunton that the substantial ruins which had still been standing when Girdler drew his sketch of the parish forty years earlier were gone by the end of the seventeenth century.

Dunton mentioned the infirmary of the Royal Hospital which stood outside the wall nearer to the river and 'in which also the stewart of the hospital and his family dwelt'. This was to be extended in 1701 and it survives today, much altered, as a Garda depot on St John's Road West.

Justice continued to be administered at Kilmainham, with even a late outlawry case being brought there in the year of his visit. Dunton turned his attention to this aspect of the area, as well as to its association with the milling of cloth:

> In this town stands the jail and session-house of the county of Dublin, with one of the same family of the three-legged gentleman [gallows] at Tyburn to give malefactors their exit out of this world.
>
> Here is a large ground plot called in for manufactory, but that is at a stand as they say by reason that England is so much disgusted at the great progress they make in working up wool.[17]

A short time before Dunton visited Dublin the gallows had been moved to Kilmainham from its former position north of the river near what is now Parkgate Street. There, presumably, it had rather spoiled the effect of the new approach to the Phoenix Park. At the close of the seventeenth century there were sketched a number of views of Dublin from the Phoenix Park, showing not only Islandbridge but also the Royal Hospital. In these works Sidney's bridge, erected in 1578 and destroyed only at the end of the eighteenth century, is clearly visible.[18]

Also at the turn of the century Lord Galway, one of the lords justices, persuaded the authorities of the Royal Hospital to permit him a right of way between their buildings and the river. This made it easier for him to travel between the north quays in Dublin and his home beyond Islandbridge. Although known as 'Lord Galway's walk', the line of this right of way was in 1753 depicted as a roadway by Tudor and on it that artist drew a coach and four. In fact, as we shall see below, Lord Galway's walk came to be regarded locally as a public thoroughfare and attempts by the governors of the Royal Hospital to close it were resisted.[19]

As the eighteenth century opened, Kilmainham once again found at its heart a major military institution with monastic overtones. Not only was the central quadrangle surrounded by 'piazzas', which might pass for cloisters, but accommodation was reserved for single men and these were obliged to attend religious services. A Knight Hospitaller might have felt at home there, although it must be said that the new pensioners were generally of a more humble standing than many of those who had lived nearby in former times. Later, however, the Royal Hospital was to be associated not only with old men but also with the social life of younger officers and the commander-in-chief of the forces came to use it as his official residence.

The holy well of St John

Many springs were regarded as sacred places even before the coming of the saints who were later associated with them. These springs, or 'wells' as they were also known, were the site of druidic or other pre-Christian ceremonies. Although in the 'Account' of Maignenn there is no reference to a holy well at Kilmainham, the first story about him in the 'Account' associates the saint with the cure of an eye disease. The power to heal eyes was one of the chief characteristics of pre-Christian wells.[1]

In the voluminous records of the Royal Hospital from 1684 the local holy well rates scarcely a mention, with one important exception which will be considered below. If these records and the 'Account' were our only sources we might not notice that such a well had ever existed or that, like so many other wells, it was the site of frequent and fervent gatherings.

Certain customs which are associated with the sites of holy wells were mentioned in the context of Kilmainham in a letter to John Alen, which was written just three years before the dissolution of the priory of St John. This letter alerts us to the fact that it had long been a popular place of assembly and also to the fact that the bishop of Meath saw fit to preach there on Palm Sunday. Thus, in 1538, Archbishop Browne of Dublin complained about Doctor Staples, bishop of Meath, that

> He hath not only sithens [since] that time by pen, as you know his wont full well, railed and raged against me, calling me heretic and beggar, with other rabulous revilings, as I have written unto my Lord, which I am ashamed to rehearse; but also, on Palm Sunday at afternoon in Kilmainham, where the stations and also pardons be now as bremely [loudly, shrilly] used as ever they were, yet cannot I help it, because the place is exempt, but I trust it is not so exempt but that the king's commandment might take place there, as you know he is highly bolstered.[2]

Browne's description of Kilmainham as being 'exempt' probably refers to the fact that the priory was beyond the reach of ordinary diocesan authority, rather than to the existence of any ancient monastic right of sanctuary. In any event, he would soon obtain royal sanction to unite under his own diocesan supervision the parish church of St John, Kilmainham, with the churches of St James and St Catherine in Dublin City.[3]

At the time of their disagreement, Browne and Staples were vying for the approval of King Henry VIII, in connection with his dispute with the

Pope, and the rivalry had led to Browne personally going to Kilmainham to hear Staples make this sermon 'in the pulpit'. It is not stated if the pulpit was inside the church mentioned above or if it was outdoors, as was the case of one other pulpit at another St John's Well. From the related records and correspondence it appears that the Pope's 'pardons' [indulgences] were on Palm Sunday, 1538, hanging in the church of Kilmainham, 'according to that day of station before time used there for the maintenance of the Bishop of Rome's authority'. There is some evidence from elsewhere that the Holy See attached indulgences to such devotions.[4]

Between Browne's complaint and the first recorded mention of a well at Kilmainham two centuries passed. Before the close of the sixteenth century, however, practices associated with another well in Dublin were described. This was St Patrick's Well, found about where Nassau Street now is. In 1592 it was said of it that,

> Upon that day [17 March] thither they will run by heaps, men, women and children, and there, first performing certain superstitious ceremonies, they drink of the water; and when they are returned to their own homes, for nine days after, they will sit and tell what wonderful things have been wrought by the operation of the water of St Patrick's Well.[5]

The penal laws which began to be introduced from the end of the seventeenth century drove catholics to attend traditional sites of popular devotion, paricularly as they were deprived of more conventional places of worship. Some catholics still hoped that James III, 'the Pretender', might yet become king and relieve them from oppression and restore their property. In 1710 we find a bill preferred to the grand jury at Kilmainham

> against one Cusack, a tanner of the aforesaid place, for saying (as the Pretender's men were taken to prison there) who would blame them for endeavouring to get estates if they could, for that fellows that came over in leathern breeches and wooden shoes, now rides in their coaches.[6]

In 1710, parliament turned its attention to a gathering at 'St John's Well'. Members expressed their concern at a 'tumultuous, dangerous and unlawful assembly' of an estimated 10,000 'papists', who were gathered from several parts of the kingdom, 'under pretence of religious worship, at a place called St John's Well, within fourteen miles of the city, to the great disturbance and hazard of the public peace'. Various writers have taken this to intend Kilmainham, ignoring the distance mentioned. It seems more likely that the commons had in mind St John's Well at Warrenstown near

Dunshaughlin, Co. Meath. As the penal laws made it difficult, if not impossible, for catholics to resort to church, the people showed their defiance by
assembling in large numbers to hear mass at the sites of holy wells. Some of
the old flagstones served as altars.[7]

The faithful of Dublin who crowded into unsuitable premises to hear
mass surreptitiously did so at some risk to their lives. A number of buildings
collapsed under the strain of supporting large numbers and people were
killed. It may be no coincidence that the first explicit reference to St John's
Well at Kilmainham is found during this period, in the records of the Royal
Hospital, when many catholics may have preferred to express their devotion out-of-doors.[8]

Before considering this and certain other references to the well which
are found in the minutes of the Royal Hospital and in books which appeared in the nineteenth century, it may be noted that the authors generally
were members of a protestant culture which had little or no sympathy for
Gaelic society and for its practices. In fairness, as we shall see, it must also be
said that some catholic bishops were also unhappy about their faithful congregating on what were probably pre-Christian gathering sites and there
being engaged in disorderly or unbecoming behaviour.

The early ethos of the Royal Hospital is symbolised by the oldest standing military headstone at Kilmainham. It is for one Corporal William Proby,
who died in 1700 and who is said to have fought in the Williamite wars.
That many of the first old soldiers who found refuge in the hospital were
survivors of the bitter conflict between William and James may be seen
from references in the records to veterans who lost limbs at the battles of
Aughrim and Mullingar and at the siege of Derry.[9]

With such soldiers as inmates and others of similar background in administration it is not surprising to find that the hospital was soon pervaded
by a spirit of religious intolerance. Dissenters who would not come to service were threatened with expulsion and even those who were employed to
do the most menial jobs were generally expected to conform strictly. This is
clear from a remarkable entry in the minutes for 9 April 1699:

> The committee having considered the necessitous condition of Rose
> Reynor, lately discharged out of the hospital as being a papist, and it
> appearing she was a laborious servant there as one of the nurses and
> her husband having been a protestant and a trumpet[er] in the army
> and lost a son in his present majesty's service, they recommend her
> case to the consideration of the gov. and in regard there are several
> nasty and bed-ridden men in the hospital who the committee think
> may be most fitly placed by themselves at one end of the upper
> gallery in No.(1) and (2) that will need particular looking after, and
> the said Rose Reynor being willing to undertake the same at the

allowance of 40 s[hillings] a year instead of £6.10[s] allowed to other
nurses, the committee do recommend the same to the consideration
of the governor.[10]

On 17 June 1739 it was agreed by the governors that 'no part of the
hospital lands ought to be set to any Roman Catholic tenant' and this same
day we find a reference in the minutes to 'a well near Kilmainham frequented by numbers of superstitious persons', the area being 'by day and
night full of idle and disorderly people'. The governors thought that the use
by the public of the area made the adjacent field almost useless for grazing
cattle.[11] This was the first occasion on which they minuted a reference to
the well and it seems, from purusing the records, that the well was regarded
as being effectively a parcel of commonage outside of their control, rather
than portion of the property of the hospital. The lands were not enclosed by
high walls as they are today and the hospital sat in open country. It was
sketched about this time by Charles Brooking.

Intrusions onto the property of the hospital continued. Many Dubliners
regarded the old cemetery as a public burial place and the special 'walk' or
right-of-way, which had been opened originally for Lord Galway, was being used by all and sundry as a short-cut from Islandbridge to Dublin. Attempts by the hospital to assert what they regarded as their right to close off
their lands led to a successful legal challenge by local residents and to an
exhibition of popular passion following the judgement, when walls and
enclosures other than those challenged in court were 'insolently and mali-
ciously thrown down'.[12]

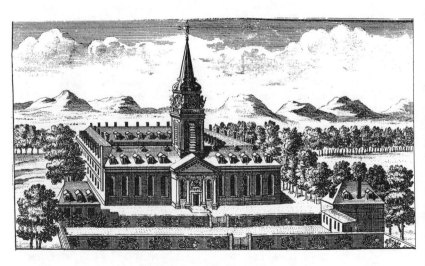

10 Charles Brooking, Royal Hospital, 1728.

These events were to be recalled in 1795 by the Royal Hospital's surveyor, Sir John Trail. That year, on the eve of St John's Eve, he signed a long report containing his version of the recent history of the area around St John's Well and the nearby cemetery. No doubt Trail took a personal interest in the matter, for he himself was a resident of Islandbridge. He had earlier been appointed high sheriff of Dublin and had designed the new prison of Kilmainham, which stood on Gallows' Hill. A map or plan, on which points mentioned in his account were marked, appears to have been lost. But looking at Rocque's map of 1756, which was discussed earlier on p. 40 and which is reproduced on p. 50 below, 'D' may have been the dark rectangle at the top of the arc opposite the end of the western avenue of the Royal Hospital and 'F' one of the rectangles at the bottom of that arc. In his report of 1795 Trail wrote that ·

Between fifty and sixty years ago a man of the name of Flanagan built a small hut or cabin at 'D' on the side of the road and brink of St John's Well, which at this time was much frequented by credulous devotees who believed the holy water efficacious in washing away at once offences and disorders, and Flanagan like many [of] his superiors turned piety into profit: by his wife's assiduity in furnishing vessels to dip in or drink the water he was soon enabled to enlarge his house and extend his trade to the sale of ale, spirits and cakes etc.

Flanagan died about 34 or 35 years ago, having two sons – one of them a mason [later 'obliged to fly from the kingdom to avoid prosecution'], the other a gardener, both of them riotous, worthless fellows – and when in their occupation 'the House of St John's Well', by which appellation the house built by their father, and already mentioned, was universally known, became a notorious receptacle for the vile and vicious.

At the time Flanagan the father made his settlement good at John's Well, the House of Gallows' Hill at 'F' was inhabited by one Andrew Cullen, a farmer, dairy-man and publican [who] ... held from the master of the Royal Hospital the burying ground and fields in dispute at an acreable rent. At this time there was a gate and kind of stile at the entrance to the burying ground and Cullen would not suffer a grave to be opened or the ground broken until paid what he called his fee, *viz*: from 3*d*. to 1*s*. in proportion to the size of the coffin and the circumstances or appearance of those who attended the interment.

While this practice continued Cullen made money and the burial ground was not, as at present, an offensive and dangerous nuisance. Yet it was productive of much mischief from the vast crowds of

people who on certain eves and days, and I may say nights, assembled there and at the well: the ditches and hedges of the contiguous
lands could not be preserved: the nights and days set apart for devotion were here perverted to riot and debauchery and generally ter-
minated by the perpetration of crimes most offensive to society.

When General Dilkes became master of the Royal Hospital
[c.1759] he endeavoured to put a stop to these pernicious nocturnal
revels. He applied to the magistrates who frequently attended and
dispersed them and he completely enclosed the burying ground by
the walls 'T', 'U', 'V'. He levelled the graves, removed the headstones and even interred the ancient monument of Brian Boru in the
same grave which tradition says contains the royal dust of that renowned Irish king and saint. This had the desired effect: the frequent
compliments to the departed friends by decorating their graves with
garlands, and the worshipping of Brian's monument ceased; these
objects of respect and adoration were removed and John's Well lost
much of its wonted powerful attraction.

Trail says that the 'truly religious' applauded the general's actions, while
'the idle, riotous and superstitious condemned it as sacrilegious'. He la-
ments the fact that the hospital's attempts to maintain exclusive boundaries
had been subsequently foiled by legal action and by the actions of a mob
which took the judgement not only as a signal to re-open the 'walk' through
hospital lands but also as a licence to throw down the walls of Bully's Acre.[13]

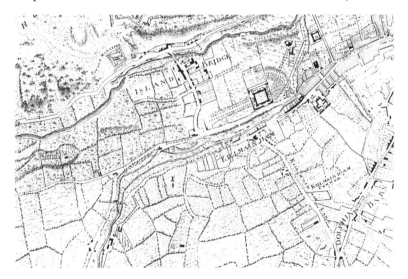

11 Section of Rocque's map of Dublin and suburbs, 1756,
from Kilmainham Common to Islandbridge.

The gathering of a large number of people at popular holy wells, where drinking and faction fighting had become a problem, continued to disturb some of the catholic bishops. On 11 December 1786 Archbishop Carpenter directed that a prohibition be read from the altars against 'resorting to a place on the Circular Road, to which they give the name of St John's Well and there under pretext of devotion occasion many scandalous enormities, not only disgraceful to religion but to civil society'. The prohibition was delivered the week before the celebration of Saint Maignenn's feast day, which fell on 18 December, and this suggests that it used to be customary for crowds to assemble at the well in midwinter, in addition to midsummer. Another letter was read from the altars the following June, urging that no Roman Catholic should encourage people to frequent 'the well at the Royal Hospital, commonly called St John of Jerusalem's Well, on or about the 24th inst. – by erecting tents, by their presence or otherwise, under pain of disobedience to the church'. Carpenter was sympathetic to Gaelic culture but was also active in supervising a range of recently authorised parish chapels, which required the support of the faithful, and the second letter specifically urged people to attend chapel instead of going to the well.[14]

Such strictures had a limited effect and revelry continued at the well of St John. About 1790 Joseph L'Estrange and three other medical students went from Dublin to Kilmainham to celebrate St John's Eve. L'Estrange, a catholic lad from Westmeath, later recalled this visit for the *Salmagundi*, a Dublin periodical:

> We took our seats in the jingle, and rattled along at the risk of our necks over the broken and uneven road until we came to the scene of mirth and eccentricity. The town of tents and the noise and music, with the bustle of the crowd – men, women and children – exceeded anything of the kind I had ever before seen or imagined; the number and variety of the booths, with their din of cymbals and big drums, each striving to drown the noise of his neighbour in the outrageous clamour of his own, were all so very many sources of excitement and wonder to my young and ardent mind, unused to such sights. My companions, though inured to all the pleasures of the metropolis, seemed to enter into the spirit of the place with feelings scarcely less subdued than my own, and we began to cast about for amusement.
>
> The first thing that particularly caught my attention was a little, old, hard-featured chap, apparently in a most agitated state of intoxication, seated on the ground against the wall with a board on his lap, on which he twirled a pea with three thimbles in inimitable style, pouring out with surprising dexterity a bundle of proverbs as an encouragement to the crowd around him.

When L'Estrange lost money to this trickster the medical student and his friends simply got it back by force and went off to a nearby 'magnificent caravan, where wonderful, artificial and magical figures were to be exhibited'. This appears to have been some kind of a magic-lantern show but the lads were prevented from seeing it when the structure collapsed. Relieved of his silk handkerchief by a pick-pocket, L'Estrange and his colleagues then retired to a tent for drinks. Inside, at one end, was a blind fiddler on a three-legged stool and, at the other end, a lame fiddler on an empty barrel. In the dancing which ensued one of the students was embroiled in a fist fight over some woman whom he kissed.

L'Estrange, who had subsequently become a journalist instead of a doctor, recalled in 1834 that his visit to St John's Well ended after midnight with a 'sackem-up', when he and his colleagues disinterred the body of a poor old man from the cemetery and brought it to a dissecting room in their hospital. This was a reminder that, until shortly before he wrote, doctors had no legitimate means of obtaining corpses for dissection and that there was a brisk business in body-snatching.[15]

The date at which the well of Kilmainham became known as 'St John's Well' is unknown. Such wells are often called by the name of the local 'patron' and Ó Danachair has written that 'it has been suggested that the well at Kilmainham was originally St Maighnen's, later changed to St John's', but he cites no source for this statement. We cannot say if the knights renamed an existing holy well for St John and then ensured that it was visited at the midsummer feast of the nativity of their patron, rather than at the midwinter feastday of Maignenn.[16]

In 1204 King John commanded that fairs be established and continue annually for eight days at Donnybrook, Waterford, Limerick and 'at the bridge of St John the Baptist'. This has recently been taken to have been intended to refer to Kilmainham. If it did so, it suggests that midsummer celebrations were deliberately fostered there by the Normans. However, there is no evidence that the bridge across the Liffey at Kilmainham was ever known as 'the bridge of St John'. Although it was regarded as being 'ancient' by the late sixteenth century, as we have seen, it is also not known if it had been constructed by 1204. Gilbert appears to have taken the reference to indicate a bridge at Drogheda, in which town a June fair was held into modern time, as well as a May fair. But there appears never to have been a bridge of St John in that town.[17]

St John's Eve

Before continuing with the story of St John's Well and of the Kilmainham area in general, it is useful to take stock of what we have learnt of the well from Sir John Trail and other sources and to place the customs associated with it in the wider context of traditional celebrations

From Browne in 1538 we saw that 'the stations' were long kept at Kilmainham on Palm Sunday and other days. From the efforts of the catholic archbishop of Dublin to curtail worship there in 1786 and 1787, it appears that crowds assembled at the well both in midsummer and in midwinter. One may speculate that the older observance was that in December, when the feast of Maignenn was celebrated, but this is the only reference to it which I have found and the weather in June no doubt tended to attract greater crowds to the exposed site.

From L'Estrange we saw that the clergy may indeed have had just cause for concern about the behaviour of their faithful on such occasions. From Trail in 1795 we learnt that the well was 'much frequented by credulous devotees who believed the holy water efficacious in washing away at once offences and disorders' - and that there were 'vast crowds of people who on certain eves and days, and I may say nights, assemble there'. We also heard that graves used to be decorated with 'garlands' and that the shaft known as Brian Boru's monument was 'worshipped'. This reference to 'garlands' may indicate that at Kilmainham people also celebrated 'Garland Sunday' or Lughnasa.[1]

The suggestion that the holy water of the well was considered efficacious not only in washing away manifest disorders but also in purging sin and its burden of guilt is one to which the Irish word 'iccaidh' is relevant. This word, which will be considered again below in Appendix C, reflects a particular view of healing which integrates the physical and the spiritual. Cogan reminds us, in discussing another St John's Well on the border between Tipperary and Offaly: 'It was not the water, of itself, that performed the miracle, but God used the water as an instrument, either to reward the lively faith of the pilgrim, or through the intercession of the patron saint'.[2]

Trail's reference to people 'worshipping' the monument of Brian Boru may be no more than a piece of protestant contempt for 'credulous' catholic attitudes toward statuary and images. Perhaps people kissed or rubbed the shaft, just as pilgrims on midsummer's eve kissed a carved figure at Streul Wells.[3]

It is possible that some special custom was associated with the curious shaft, which itself might have replaced or been transformed from a standing stone connected to some earlier fertility rite. There is circumstantial evidence to support such a hypothesis, although it is of such recent vintage that it may simply reflect later licence.

Thus, in 1786 we have the archbishop decrying 'scandalous enormities' and in 1795 Trail lamenting 'debauchery' at Bully's Acre. In 1843 Burton noted that the decoration on the shaft is 'what lady-language terms a true lover's knot, but really an ancient emblem of eternity'. Harbison describes the west face as 'a sunken panel, bearing a curious interlace which tightens as it descends before terminating in two pendants with circular 'bosses' at the bottom' and Weir has stated boldly that 'such knot-figures represented Lust in Romanesque sculpture, appearing frequently on capitals of doorways'. However, Harbison avoids endorsing such an interpretation. The name of the

12 Granite shaft (west face) at Bully's Acre.

cemetery itself may be explained in a number of ways and one of these derives from an archaic meaning of 'bully' which is 'lover'. There lingered a belief that on such nights as St John's Eve those who had atoned by visiting wells could incur no further guilt by their actions on the site.[4]

The revels at Kilmainham were not the only ones in which the population of Dublin liked to engage. Disorder was such that the lord mayor of the city himself felt it necessary from time to time to ban such celebrations. Thus, for example, in 1742 he banned all bonfires on midsummer eve and Saint Peter's Eve.[5]

Joyce tells us that St Maelruan's patron or 'pattern' was celebrated at Tallaght every year on 7 July , although the saint's name became corrupted in time to 'Moll Rooney'. However, the event became such a nuisance, 'owing to drunkenness and debauchery', that it was suppressed in 1874 and the degeneration of this pattern was considered by Joyce to be 'unfortunately only typical of others throughout the country, which explains why so many of them have been discontinued through the influence of the clergy and others'.[6] He adds of Tallaght:

The proceedings consisted in making a kind of effigy, supposed to represent the saint, and carrying it about from house to house in procession, headed by a fiddler or piper. The occupants of each house then came out as they were visited, and danced to the music after which a collection was made to be spent on drink. Few went to bed that night; many slept in ditches on the way home, and drinking, dancing and fighting went on intermittently till morning

In June 1813 Crofton Croker, who was hostile to customs associated with holy wells, visited the lake of Gougane Barra in West Cork and there encountered an emotional throng, gathered as usual at midsummer:

It was not without difficulty that we forced our way through the crowd on the shore of the lake, to the walls of the chapels on the island, where we stood amid an immense concourse of people: the interior of the cells were filled with men and women in various acts of devotion, almost all of them on their knees; some with hands uplifted, prayed in loud voices, using considerable gesticulation, and others, in a less noisy manner, rapidly counted the beads of their rosary, or, as it is called by the Irish peasant, their 'pathereen', with much apparent fervour; or as a substitute for beads, they threw from one hand into the other, small pebbles to mark the number of prayers they had repeated, whilst such of them as were not furnished with other means kept their reckoning by cutting a notch on their cudgel, or a piece of stick provided for the purpose ...

Within, the well was crowded to excess, probably seven or eight persons, some with their arms, some with their legs thrust down into the water, exhibiting the most disgusting sores and shocking infirmities.

Croker refers to copies of a prayer being sold on the day. These ended: 'N.B. You must be careful to avoid all excess in drinking [and] dancing in tents, for it is impossible characters can find favour in the sight of God, such as these'. Nevertheless, 'drunken men and the most depraved women mingled with those whose ideas of piety brought them to this spot' and he observes that, 'whiskey, porter, bread and salmon were sold in booths or tents resembling a gypsy encampment'. He also mentions a long stone set up on the island, with a long inscription stating the number of prayers to be repeated at each of the cells. In 1818 the local bishop proscribed the practices there.[7]

In 1943 the Folklore Department at University College Dublin conducted a special national survey concerning the observance of St John's Eve. The results indicated that the tradition of celebrating around bonfires on 23 June appeared to have died out in Dublin, while it lingered on in counties such as Meath and Westmeath.[8] This was not surprising as it has principally been a rural festival of the summer solstice when crops are fairly advanced and people are solicitous for good results. Even today in Ireland such fires are still lit at midsummer.

The survey of 1943 found that central to the tradition as it was remembered in the mid-twentieth century were bonfires, lit usually at a crossroads. Around these there was prayer and dance. The fact that the celebrations began on the evening before and not the evening of the saint's day is itself indicative of ancient origins when the reckoning of time was fundamentally lunar, being counted in nights rather than days, and thus festivals began when darkness fell on what now is considered the previous day.

Where people or animals may once have been burnt on the 'bone-fires', more recently youths and beasts ran through them or over them – 'for good luck'. The 'most daring of girls' leapt through and were 'talked of all over the area till next St John's Eve'.

Thus Thomas Lawless, aged eighty, reported in 1943 that 'it used to be said that if a young boy or girl danced through the embers they would be married before the year would be out'. If the boy failed to make it he would become a priest and the girl a nun. Was this merely a measure of their perceived potency or something more ancient, a distant folk-memory of sacrificial victims whose lives were once literally devoted to the divinity?

The survey of 1943 found that there was rivalry to have the biggest blaze and we recall how Kilmainham was honoured when Maelruain told Maignenn that the fire there would enjoy a special distinction.

St John's Eve was believed to be a night when the fairies went travelling from the raths and they would be scared off by fire. One witness in 1943 claimed that he himself had seen the fairy hunt doing rounds of the fire.

From the bonfire when it had burnt away, people took home cinders or embers to put among the crops or in the cow-shed or well or garden for good luck. 'Old people brought tongs' to take away their piece of the fire and might place a coal under the churn 'so that the butter would not be spirited away', said witnesses in 1943. Cinders were also put into one's own fireplace, a practice in which one may discern a faint trace of the belief on Inishmurray that all fires were kindled from a central source. Meath itself, after all, was the location of the primal fire of Uisneach, 'which spread its blaze tar cethri hairde Herend'.[9] Those over ninety who kept in their possession an ember from the bonfires of St John's Eve would die happy, it was said. With so many people removing embers and ashes we recall an image of the fire of St Brighid which left no ashes no matter how much it burnt.[10]

Such was the status of the feast of St John the Baptist that into the nineteenth century it was observed as a *dies non*, or non-sitting day, by the several courts of justice.[11]

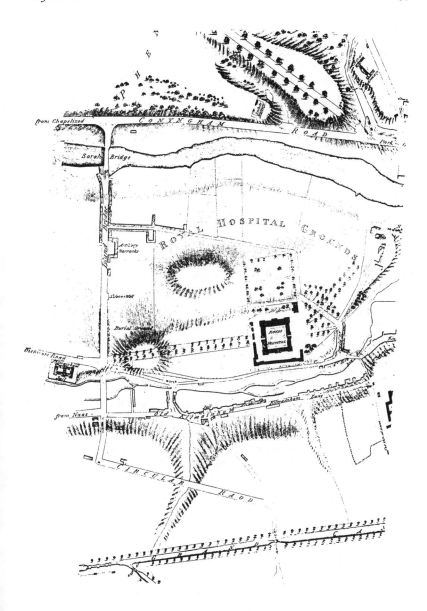

13 Survey by Thomas Campbell, showing St John's Well at its old location, AD 1811.
Also shown are the sites of the old and new gaols, the burial ground
of Bully's Acre and the Grand Canal.

New Kilmainham

Up on the ridge, between the avenue of the Royal Hospital and the River Camac, ran the old highway to the west of Ireland. Down below, on the south side of the Camac, ran the main road to Munster. Along the latter route stretched the small town of Kilmainham, of which Girdler has left us a rough sketch in the plan of the parish which he drew about 1657. It may also be seen in crude outline on Bernard de Gomme's map of 1673. The town appears to have grown up around the main gate of the outer enclosure or manor-close of the old priory which, as we have seen, McNeill says faced the common green. The common was shown by Rocque on his map of 1756 reproduced above at p. 50, as lying to the south-east of this settlement. Each year there was held here a summer fair which, like the celebrations associated with the well beyond the brow of the ridge, often degenerated into drunkenness and brawling. In 1747 an attempt was made to suppress it. Soldiers were called out when crowds gathered for races on the common and in the confrontation which followed a number of people were shot dead. In 1751 the protestant Liberty Boys and the catholic Ormond Party assembled at Kilmainham for St James' Fair and were said to have remained in riotous disorder until nightfall.[1]

Commotions such as these cannot have pleased the families who lived in the old town in the mid-eighteenth century. They included that of Simon Bradstreet, a lawyer of great eminence who in 1759 became the first Baronet of Kilmainham. The house which he occupied stood across the Camac from Kilmainham Mills and was pulled down as recently as the 1960s. Lost in the demolition was a statue of William Shakespeare which may have been sculpted by Peter Scheemakers, a foremost eighteenth-century scuptor who made a similar memorial to the writer which is in Westminster Abbey. When this statue in Kilmainham was rediscovered about 1911 it caused something of a stir in Dublin. The house which the Bradstreet family occupied had been built about 1725 by John Fitzpatrick, a prominent Dublin attorney. It was nothing new for lawyers to live in Kilmainham, for many judges and other leading members of the legal profession had been connected with the Knights Hospitallers. The knights had also kept a prison. By the eighteenth-century the local gaol and associated county court-house, where people were 'justiced', both stood on the main street of the old town of Kilmainham.[2]

Kilmainham was, as we noted above, one of the places where those who were sentenced to death met their fate. The other was St Stephen's Green. Rocque's map of 1756 shows, as we discovered too, that there was a space between the end of the western avenue of the Royal Hospital, still then the only entrance to that institution, and the roads west to Inchicore and north to Islandbridge. The area around where those roads met was also considered a parcel of common ground, stretching as it did from the well of St John by Bully's Acre to beyond the site of scaffold. Since the place of execution had been moved from a point north of the river at the end of the seventeenth century, this elevated part of Kilmainham had come to be known as 'Gallows' Hill'. Unfortunates were hanged there in large numbers. Nearby stood a windmill which was destroyed in a freak accident in 1763 when its iron works heated during a fierce storm.[3]

Any of the idle or curious who in June 1785 gathered here to witness the hanging of five condemned men certainly went home with an extraordinary tale to tell their friends.

> The execution on Saturday last was, by an accident, rendered distressing to every person capable of feeling for the misfortunes of their fellow creatures. In about a minute after the five unhappy criminals were turned off, the temporary gallows fell down, and on its resurrection it was found necessary to suffer three of the unhappy wretches to remain half strangled on the ground until the other two underwent the sentence of the law, when they in their turn were tied up and executed.[4]

At this time people were sentenced to death and to transportation for a wide variety of crimes, the latter fate being lamented in a local ballad:

> Lord Altham is a very bad man,
>   As all the neighbours know,
> For driving white Roger from Kilmainham lands,
>   We all to Virginy[a] must go.

The Annesley family, of which the lords Altham were members, was long associated with Inchicore. Those who had attempted to take the family's beast may have been lucky to escape with their lives for, at the quarter sessions held in old Kilmainham in May 1787, one person was sent for hanging because he had stolen seven sheep and another because he took a gelding. A man who stole a brass candlestick, a pair of boots and a copper kettle got off more lightly when he was merely transported. The same penalty awaited two women who had taken some items of clothing. Another popular punishment involved flogging and one John Byrne was whipped from Kilmainham to Mount-Brown for hiding himself in a shop.[5]

However, such severe punishment did not deter everyone from felony and criminals remained active in the area. The government decided that a

new county gaol and court-house would be erected up at Gallows' Hill.
The work of building the gaol was already underway when, in October
1787, it was reported that,

> Kilmainham road continues to be infested by the same dangerous
> gang who have preyed upon the unsuspecting traveller these two
> months past. Tuesday evening, a carrier from Mountrath was stopped
> on the new road a little beyond the Red Lion, by a number of
> ruffians, who after plundering his car of seventeen pounds of congou
> tea in separate parcels, a large bundle of ribbons and nine yards of
> muslin, ordered him to drive on, threatening to follow and blow his
> brains out if he made the least noise for half an hour.[6]

One kind person, who in 1789 attempted to show his sympathy for the
inmates of the old prison at Kilmainham, found to his cost that being locked
up did not put an end to the activities of wrongdoers:

> A gentleman passing by Kilmainham gaol put his hand into the bars
> with some half-pence for the relief of the prisoners, when one of the
> audacious hardened villains took hold of his wrist, whilst another
> with a razor, swore he would cut off his hand if he did not instantly
> deliver his purse, upon which the gentleman gave the miscreant a
> guinea and a crown, all the money he had about him.[7]

It is scarcely surprising to find that if one man might dispense charitable
donations through the bars of the gaol which faced directly onto the street,
then others were quite prepared to pass less worthy objects through the
windows. These included instruments to secure the escape of prisoners and
such substantial quantities of alcohol that inmates were said to be often
roaring drunk from early in the day. The old gaol was in an unwholesome
and bad situation with narrow sunken cells underground but the new gaol,
by contrast, was built on elevated ground for ventilation. It was designed by
the local architect, John Trail. On 12 August 1796 the first prisoners were
conveyed there from the old gaol and Faulkner's *Dublin Journal* reported
that the new institution, 'for safety, healthfulness, convenience and com-
pactness is said to be superior to any prison in Europe'. The sites of both the
old and the new gaol were marked by Campbell on his survey of 1811,
which is reproduced above at p. 57.

Before long overcrowding and dampness were to spoil the new gaol's
reputation. Outside it for over two decades executions continued to take
place publicly. From the 1820s the number of hangings declined considerably and a place of execution was created inside the prison. Local folklore
has it that the hangman had a tunnel through which he might avoid the

14 Sarah Bridge, erected at Islandbridge 1791.

public on his way to work from his house across Inchicore Road. Over the solid entrance door of the new gaol was placed a frieze depicting five entwined serpents or dragons, which became known as 'the devils of Kilmainham'. These are thought to be the demons of crime restrained by the chains of law and justice. They also recall the reptile by which Maignenn was plagued.[8]

Another improvement to the Kilmainham and Inchicore areas was the construction of the Grand Canal. On 15 April 1773 Earl Harcourt, the lord lieutenant, had been escorted to the south of old Kilmainham by a squadron of cavalry and had laid the foundation stone of the first lock. Between the canal and the old town ran the new Circular Road from Dublin. This passed by the western entrance to the Royal Hospital and effectively brought the whole area closer to the city. As houses came to be built in the vicinity of the new gaol and court-house the district was to become known as 'New Kilmainham', thus distinguishing it from the old and somewhat decayed village below. To carry the new Circular Road across the Liffey there was erected in 1791 at Islandbridge the elegant 'Sarah Bridge'. It stood slightly downstream from the old bridge, which had been damaged by a flood.[9]

As the population of Dublin increased poor families used the new road to resort in great numbers to the ancient cemetery of 'Bully's Acre'. This was not regulated as later cemeteries such as those at Goldenbridge and Glasnevin would be. At the time Catholics were not allowed to keep their own places of burial and they resorted to traditional sites against the law. In 1766, at quarter sessions in Kilmainham, Sir Edward Newenham had delivered himself of some pertinent comments in the course of his charge to the grand jury of County Dublin:

I must observe to you, that the law allows of no burials at those remnants of Popish bigotry and superstition, decayed abbeys or monasteries: of course they are proper subjects for presentments.[10]

The grand jury did make periodic efforts to have the Royal Hospital take charge more effectively of Bully's Acre and in the last decade of the century they had some success. By then the cemetery had come to be regarded as a disgrace,

from the great number of dead bodies carelessly left there, many of them not interred, for the sprinkling of earth thrown over them is insufficient to conceal from the eye the coffins and shells which contain them. Danger to the health of the public is to be apprehended. In this once highly venerated repository for the dead, but now a common on the verge of the highway, scenes shocking to minds capable of reflection and horrid to relate are frequently exhibited: swine devouring human bodies which are in the most pernicious state of putrefaction and the torn remains of males and females left exposed to public view.[11]

Following certain representations from the public a grand jury held that the Royal Hospital was responsible for the area and it was agreed by its governors to appoint a keeper of the cemetery. On the eve of St John's Eve in 1795 the hospital's surveyor, Sir John Trail, signed a lengthy report which,

15 Font of St John's Well, *c.*1795-1845. Now at Order of Malta, Clyde Road, Dublin.

as we saw above, contained his version of the then recent history of the area. This was one part of a review of the administration of the hospital which then took place. With the repeal of most of the penal laws catholics were to be admitted to the institution in increasing numbers during the nineteenth century and a catholic chaplain was allowed to work there. Financial support for the Royal Hospital was put on a firmer footing and physical improvements were undertaken which included, notably, the construction of a substantial perimeter wall. Also erected, adjacent to St John's Well and at the corner of Bully's Acre, was a tower which served as a conduit for water to the Royal Hospital. This is clearly visible in both Ashford's and Malton's fine views of Islandbridge and Dublin, painted about 1795. Both it and the holy well were subsequently swept away by the cutting of a passage for the new railway.[12]

With walls being erected in 1795, the opportunity was taken to tidy up St John's Well itself and its waters were directed into a granite basin or font. This was placed in a special structure made of granite blocks, at least eight feet high. The basin and some blocks survive elsewhere today, as we shall see below. A survey of the Kilmainham area in 1811 by Thomas Campbell, which is reproduced above at p. 57 clearly shows the location of the well as it was contained after 1795.[13]

> It was a neat little fountain, in a crescent-shaped recess about twenty
> feet wide, at the side of the road, all formed of cut granite block and
> benches, where one could sit and eat the oaten cakes and butter and

16 Part of the surround of St Johns Well, *c.*1795-1845. Now at Church of St James, Dublin.

water-cress, and if so minded, drink the water out of the little mugs, of which there was a quantity. Often and often I enjoyed a luncheon there.[14]

After the suppression of rebellion in 1798 the government moved quickly to engineer the political union of Ireland and Great Britain in one kingdom. This led to a personal dilemma for John Egan, lawyer and renowned duellist. An enormous and unusual man, he was to be mentioned frequently in Barrington's memoirs.

In 1799 Egan was appointed 'chairman of Kilmainham'. He was also a member of parliament but his judicial position as chairman of quarter sessions is said to have been almost his only source of income during a period of poverty. He was told that he would lose the post if he failed to support the union:

> As the final debate was proceeding he was seen to become more and more uneasy. At length he rose, delivered a furious speech against the union, and sat down, exclaiming: 'Ireland – Ireland, for ever! – and damn Kilmainham'.

Thereafter he was dubbed 'Damn Kilmainham', although he also enjoyed another nickname, 'Bully Egan'. He is said to have cried openly in court when sentencing prisoners.[15]

The court-house was used for other purposes besides the holding of quarter-sessions for the county. It was here that voting in general elections took place and that successful candidates for county Dublin were returned to parliament. It was regarded as a safe Tory constituency. The franchise was still very restricted in 1802. A black man, who that year was among just 143 people who voted in County Dublin and who may have been the first black ever to cast his ballot in an Irish election, met with opposition:

> A Negro having tended his vote on Tuesday last, at Kilmainham, his right of voting was much disputed by the respective agents: the Deputy determined in his favour, observing, however, that his vote was not a *fair* one.[16]

The local manor court also used the court-house. Sitting in May 1812, Leonard MacNally, seneschal of the liberties of the manor of Kilmainham, ordered the confiscation of underweight bread. Seven hundred loaves were consequently found to be 'considerably deficient' in different retail shops and were condemned and distributed to the poor.[17] That same year, west of the Royal Hospital, was erected by Messrs Willans the Hibernian Mills. Since ancient times in the area of Kilmainham there had been both flour

17 Sessions-house and gaol, Kilaminham, 1835.

mills and cloth mills and the number of these between Old Bawn and Dublin now increased as industrialists sought to capitalise on a ready supply of water from the Liffey and the Camac. In 1837 Lewis wrote that Willans had erected their mill at Kilmainham,

> for the manufacture of the finest woollen clothes, which trade they have successfully pursued, and having greatly extended their establishment, it affords employment to nearly 500 persons, for whose residence the proprietors have erected suitable dwellings, and also a place of worship for the Independent denomination.[18]

Obadiah Willan was a Yorkshire mill owner who brought with him to Kilmainham some workers from Yorkshire. Other industrialists in the area also brought over English and Scottish employees, perhaps finding them more skilled or simply more accustomed to the work ethic which was demanded than were the local people.[19]

During this period the new court-house of Kilmainham, finally completed in the second decade of the nineteenth century, was also used occasionally as a meeting place for the local freeholders. In December 1820 remarkable scenes occurred there in connection with an attempt to pass a resolution critical of the government. There was at the time controversy over the ascent of George IV. When Lord Cloncurry took the chair in the new court-house at Kilmainham a party of soldiers, with loaded muskets and drawn bayonets, emptied the room.[20]

It was also in 1820 that William Sadler painted a view upstream of the River Liffey. This shows the recently erected Wellington monument in the Phoenix Park and the Phoenix iron-works on the northern river bank. The iron-works would later become known to Dubliners as Cahill's printing works. It was here that the iron was cast for the new King's Bridge, built in 1827-8. Sadler's painting is a reminder of how rustic the scene still was around Islandbridge and Kilmainham in 1820, before the erection of the new bridge, of the nearby railway station and of the quay between Bloody Bridge and King's Bridge. In 1775, when the only entrance to the Royal Hospital had been from the west, Master Irwin had made a second entrance to it from Bow Bridge by the little street which still bears his name. This area was very decayed so in 1810 a new 'Military Road' had been opened from the quays to the north-eastern corner of the grounds. This route, known as 'the Military Road' passed over the Camac by a small bridge and both it, the Camac and the bridge are clearly visible in Sadler's painting. It was a scene which would soon be utterly transformed, with the Camac being run underground when the station was built in the 1840s.[21]

The entrance to the Military Road was through a black limestone gothic tower which was designed by Francis Johnston. It had been erected during the vice-royalty of the duke of Richmond and was known thereafter as 'Richmond Gate'. It stood where Watling Street met Bloody Bridge at what was then the western extremity of the south quays. There were wooden gates hung on the gothic tower and for some years these were closed at night to discourage 'beggars and disorderly women' from congregating on the road to the Royal Hospital. The Military Road lay approximately along part of the line of 'Lord Galway's Walk' which, as we saw earlier, was a disputed right-of-way through the grounds of the Royal Hospital.[22]

The local holy well was still being visited in large number in the first quarter of the nineteenth century. In an account, published in 1820, Thomas Cromwell wrote:

> Near Islandbridge, at which spot we arrive on the south bank of the Liffey, is St John's Well, greatly resorted to by the lower orders on the eve of its patron saint, for the purpose of drinking the waters, which are supposed to possess efficacy to cure all manner of diseases on that day. Tents are pitched, and many festivities observed on the occasion, in lieu of the old custom of lighting bonfires, (a relic, it is thought, of the pagan fire worship or Baal-tinne), which was very properly interdicted by the magistrates of Dublin. But in many country places in Ireland the bonfire is still religiously continued on this festival accompanied with several absurd and superstitious ceremonies.[23]

The following year John McGregor confirmed that 'vast numbers' still resorted to the well to drink its waters, 'which are supposed on that day to be particularly efficacious for the cure of diseases. A number of tents are pitched around'.[24]

As the area gradually developed and middle-class families moved out of the city into its surrounding districts, the continuing existence of an inadequately regulated graveyard at Kilmainham was not ignored. Amongst those who were buried at Bully's Acre were Robert Emmet, whose remains were subsequently re-interred elsewhere, and Dan Donnelly, the popular boxer who gave his name to a hollow on the Curragh of Kildare. The measures taken in 1795 to improve the condition of the graveyard had not prevented 'sackem-ups' from continuing to prey on the remains of the poor and the results were sometimes appalling. In 1820 Cromwell claimed that body-snatchers were nightly removing corpses from Bully's Acre, 'with a facility unknown in countries where feelings of reverence for the repose of the dead are stronger than in Ireland'.[25]

During the year after they won political emancipation catholics were, for the first time in centuries, provided with a proper cemetery of their own in Dublin and thus spared a repetition of earlier humiliations. This new burial ground was located near Kilmainham at Goldenbridge and was blessed on 15 October 1829. However, the old site was to be used one last time during the cholera epidemic which swept Ireland in 1832. It is said that during one six-month period over 3000 bodies were buried at Bully's Acre in unsatisfactory circumstances. When the epidemic abated the ancient cemetery was finally and effectively closed. In that year, too, the Anatomy Act was passed. This facilitated the medical profession by providing a means for the orderly acquisition of corpses.[26]

In 1834 L'Estrange noted that, although Bully's Acre was no longer in use, 'you may still behold the black spade and shovel on the white gable of 'Stafford's Public House"'.[27] It was a reminder that families who had made their way to Kilmainham to bury their deceased might find the means to do the job at the establishments of those vintners on whom they bestowed their business. One contemporary would later recall that

> At the corner of Rowserstown was Drum's public house, where those attending a funeral rested themselves and refreshed previously to digging the grave in the 'Acre'; and here, too, they were accommodated with spades and all the paraphernalia required for the preparation of the tenement.
>
> I remember that the shutters of the public houses were enriched with paintings of the pick-axes, spades, shovels, coils of rope, skulls and cross-bones – all in the language of heraldry 'proper'.[28]

18 Kilmainham pensioners.

At one point in 1834 it was thought that not only Bully's Acre but also the Royal Hospital itself might be closed by the government. A campaign, which included a petition laid before parliament by the nobility, gentlemen and merchants of Dublin, succeeded in keeping it open. *The Kilmainham Pensioner's Lament*, an illustrated poem in twenty-five verses, expressed the sentiments of that campaign. Although the old soldiers' home survived, its 'establishment' was thereafter reduced by the government, in two steps, from 400 to 140 pensioners.[29]

It was in 1834 too that the police determined to stamp out traditional festivities at Kilmainham. Recommending to parliament that measures be taken to end the Donnybrook fair, J.C. Graves wrote from police head-quarters in Dublin to a parliamentry committee on intoxication among the labouring classes:

> That little difficulty would arise to the proposed abolition has been recently proved by the suppression of the celebration of midsummer at St John's Well, near Kilmainham, where similar proceedings had been carried on for many years. This was effectively accomplished last month through the intervention of the police, with the concur-rence of the proprietor of the soil.[30]

To judge from a reference by D'Alton, which is cited in the next chapter below, this action by the police had an immediate effect. Nevertheless, just as at Donnybrook fair, popular culture soon reasserted itself in the face of official disapproval and the well continued to be visited by some people for a number of years. However, with the churches and the authorities both involved in determined efforts to eliminate what were seen as occasions for debauchery and waste, it was only a matter of time before the values of the rising middle class triumphed. In an increasingly bourgeois and industrialised society the place of fairs and holy wells in the lives of English and Irish people was limited. Where the victory of polite over popular culture has been described as 'the triumph of Lent', in the nineteenth century it might equally be depicted as 'the triumph of capitalism'.[31]

During the 1830s mill owners along the Camac united in a legal action against Counsellor Bennet of Aughfarrell, who tried to force them to pay him for the benefit of using the water in their races. Visiting the area in 1837 for the ordnance survey, Curry concluded that 'the Cammack River is the Slade More, as I supposed, and it is an artificial branch of the Liffey'. He reported that the Camac was partly created at a weir up in the Dublin hills at Aughfarrell. There Bennet had property and had attempted to stop the flow of water until such time as the merchants would pay him. He was defeated in his efforts. Curry learnt from people who lived inland from Kilmainham and along the course of the stream that, until the legal action was taken, they had not recognised the fact that the water which flowed through their parishes was the same as that known to the millers as the Camac. Curry went in search of an explanation for the origin of the name 'Camac', which had been the designation of the cutting or race at Kilmainham for many centuries before he wrote:

> One woman told me that she heard an old man, who is now dead, say that the stream first got the name of Cammack from the circumstance of the men who cut the channel being paid their wages in Cammack halfpence.[32]

The development of Kilmainham from the end of the eighteenth century was evident not only in its buildings but also in the manners and dress of those who lived there. Reflecting on this, the Revd Nathanael Burton wrote of the changes which he himself had witnessed and remembered his own arrival there in the early 1820s. He observed

> the rustic and village-like appearance of Bow Bridge and Old Kilmainham, the latter the county town, presenting even at the present [1843] in the hollow of the Cummogue [Camac] vale all the semblance of a village street, separated from the great metropolis by the hill.

Burton recalled that, in the early 1820s,

> figures might be seen in this vicinity the relics of a former genera-
> tion, whose appearance proclaimed that they were not much con-
> versant with Dublin costumes, who probably would lose their way
> in its labyrinths, and who even in High-street would be regarded a
> second time by a jaunty passenger. Men with the old brown wig and
> thick segment behind, fat hat, clothes fashioned by a travelling tailor,
> buckskin breeches – once white or yellow when in the possession of
> their forefathers ... and large buckles on their shoes; but they are
> now no more; like expiring tapers they burned more distinctly at
> their close.
>
> Here have I also seen the aged female, with snowy 'kerchief,
> '*modo Hibernico*'. on her head, enveloped in grey cloak, hobbling
> along, but seldom beyond the precincts of Kilmainham or Bow Bridge
> – in her antique basket the new-laid eggs for the 'Fogies' of the ould
> house.[33]

The people described by Burton may have had little inclination to mix
with Dubliners but they would probably have felt at ease relaxing by St
John's Well. Their way of life gradually yielded to accommodate moderni-
sation and, as the nineteenth century progressed, their familiar fields were
acquired in increasing numbers as sites on which to build houses for those
who wished to move out of the overcrowded city to a suburban home.

Victorian progress

In his *Topographical Dictionary of Ireland*, published in 1838, Samuel Lewis commented upon 'a kind of festival of considerable antiquity' which was observed on the feast day of St John at Kilmainham:

> It is much frequented by the working classes from the metropolis, for whom tents are pitched and the usual entertainments of patron days provided.[1]

This was also the period when D'Alton's great work on the history of County Dublin appeared. It contained an unflattering reference to the well which, as we saw, had been the scene of police activity shortly before D'Alton wrote. He recalled that some decades earlier 'the Roman Catholics of the diocese were very properly forbidden to frequent it', but he admitted that

> like many other less justifiable obstacles opposed to popular preju- dices, they only tended to confirm the ignorant in their proscribed observances, and intemperance and idleness continued, till within the last two years, to give annual dis-edification at St John's Well.[2]

However, it is clear that some members of the middle-class had no ob- jections to the well and one later recalled how, even as D'Alton was scorn- ing the place, it became the location for the painting of a model of the Battle of Waterloo, made by Captain William Siborne, assistant military secretary in Dublin and author of an enduring but unreliable version of the English role in that battle. His 'truly Irish work' of miniature silver soldiers and artillery, which was arrayed for the incidental amusement of anyone visiting St John's Well, was later housed in London. One of those who, in 1838, attended at Kilmainham to assist in the painting of the model later recalled the scene at the well in those last years before it was destroyed:

> bacon and cabbage, corn beef, potatoes, and pilgrims -male and fe- male – *rowling* for nuts and on merry-go-rounds; oaten-bread and Wicklow butter, watercress and the well water; with something to take off the chill if you knew how to ask for it! As you went from Kilmainham the well was exactly at the corner of 'Bully's Acre' (as the graveyard was called), and to a nicety where the centre of the railway is now. Why such a desecration of an old and venerated landmark was permitted, it is hard to say.[3]

St John's Well fell victim not only to the excavations connected with the new railway but also to revived attempts by the bishops to suppress old practices which were being abused at various holy wells around Ireland. With Catholics winning emancipation in 1829 and soon, thereafter, beginning to agitate for the repeal of the Union, unseemly behaviour in public places was not to be tolerated. The Great Famine, too, was to have a profound effect on attitudes towards older Gaelic life and on those who kept the ancient customs. It has been described by P.J. Corish, the historian of the Irish Catholic Church, as 'the great divide in the religious history of the Irish catholic community'.[4]

On the eve of the famine the old opening of the well was destroyed, as we shall see below, but a final description of it was published in 1843 by the Revd Nathanael Burton. He compared it to the pool of Siloam at Jerusalem, in which sick persons bathed at the time of Jesus, and from his account it is clear that the new basin installed in 1795 had failed to contain the local spring:

> St John's Well, the Siloam of Kilmainham, now a neglected rill, yet nature aids the blessed stream, faith once preserved it, now a wanderer; here and there it bursts above the earth, spontaneous; though in poverty, it indignantly scorns the stone front which Cunningham has raised.
>
> Nor blind, nor lame, nor halt come hither now, save a solitary mendicant, to ask an alms, or draggled drab from Chapelizod, Lucan or Maynooth, with twins of squalling urchins, fusty bag depending, with cold potatoes and scraps of bacon stored. Her idleness ... leads forth, more apt to ply the churn-dash, or pick Cork reds, the colour of her cheeks, a very denizen of hedge, or ditch, or lazy ridge.[5]

The very nature of this image is remarkable. Through the author's veneer of romantic satisfaction at a resurgent spring breaks the sweaty odour of his mother-earth figure, fecund and nourishing. The Revd Burton seems uncertain of his emotions, being half fond of and half repulsed by the hag. This well was no place for the responsible, but the poor and women still found solace by it. On the threshold of Dublin, where the guilty suffered their punishment, the innocent lived out an ancient pageant.

The elegant Victoria was reigning over a new age of mechanical progress and the cutting which brought trains from the midlands and south-west of Ireland to the newly constructed Kingsbridge Station also deprived St John's Well of its water-supply. As late as February 1845 it was not finally settled how the Great Southern and Western Railway would run from Inchicore into the city. Some wanted it to go along the line of the canal to Portobello. Others thought that it should go along the south bank of the river as far as

the bridge east of Kingsbridge, an option strongly favoured by the governors of the Royal Hospital. When the company decided upon the present
site of the terminus, to be known as Kingsbridge and later as Heuston Station, it wished to acquire land both from the artillery barracks and from the
Royal Hospital and to lay the line below the railway's present position. The
Board of Ordnance sought an unrealistic sum in compensation and, by the
time that they had been persuaded to change their mind, it was too late: a
decision had been made to go south and east of the barracks by acquiring all
necessary land from the Royal Hospital. The governors were by no means
happy about the development and feared that it would interfere with their
passage to Dublin. They pointed out that plans for the railway had been put
on public display at the General Post Office in 1844,

> exhibiting a simple line of railroad from the boundary of the park
> near St John's Well to that between it and a field the company had
> acquired from Lord Palmerstown at the King's Bridge.

On the basis of reassurances that this would involve only the loss of a
very small amount of their lands, the governors had withdrawn their threatened opposition to the passage of legislation allowing the railway company
to acquire property by compulsion if necessary. They had taken the view
that it was their duty as trustees to oppose the use of their lands for any
purpose other than those envisaged in their charter. For this reason, they
were at first incensed when it emerged that they would have to give up far
more land than they had anticipated, including all their fields on the banks
of the Liffey. They were mollified by a substantial payment.[6]

By September 1845 the railway company's engineer, Sir John McNeill,
reported that a temporary road had been made in preparation for the planned
excavation between Inchicore and Kingsbridge. By March 1846 150,000
cubic yards of earth had been removed between Inchicore and Kingsbridge
and 60,000 more remained to go. Work on the road bridge at the South
Circular Road was well in hand. In the course of the year the attitude of the
governors of the Royal Hospital changed from being 'unaccommodating'
and 'hostile' to 'very helpful' and on Monday, 3 August 1846, the line was
officially opened with a departure of guests from the station at Inchicore to
the Clonmel races. Next morning, at 9 o'clock, the public boarded the first
train to leave Kingsbridge, also bound for the Clonmel races. Passengers
were cheered out by a crowd which included some people who had been
unable to board the train, because more people wanted tickets than there
were seats.[7]

One of the consequences of the coming of the railway was the reloca-
tion of Richmond Gate which, as we saw earlier, stood at Bloody Bridge
and marked the beginning of the Military Road to the Royal Hospital. The

gate or 'tower' was thought to interfere with the approach of traffic along a new quay to the new station. D'Alton described the gate as 'a very conspicuous object the whole length of the quays'.[8]

In 1846 the governors of the hospital agreed to a proposal by the Railway Company to re-erect the gothic gateway in its present position, diagonally across their lands at the end of the western avenue facing Kilmainham Gaol. The lower portion of the Military Road was superseded after 1874 by the new quay and by St John's Road West, which runs alongside the railway from the quays to South Circular Road. A considerable amount of new land was acquired from the Royal Hospital for this purpose.[9]

Meanwhile, the cutting for the railway from Inchicore to Kingsbridge had been driven through the course of the spring supplying St John's Well, leaving high and dry the font and granite surround which had been made for it as recently as the 1790s. In his description of the train journey from Kingsbridge Station, for the writing of which he was paid £100 by the railway company, John D'Alton noted that

> The [South Circular] road from Kilmainham to Islandbridge is here carried over the railway by a bridge consisting of iron girders with cross-iron plates; the gradient here rises 1:80. Immediately before passing under the bridge at *left* was St John's Well ... the waters of the spring are now diverted from the public.[10]

Why D'Alton stressed that the well had been at the *left* (his italics) of the outward track is unknown. It appears that the font remained in place for some time on the right as one crossed over the railway bridge down to Islandbridge and it is there marked on a contemporary ordnance survey map. The space where it stood remained visible until recently, when the road to the west was widened considerably and passed over the railway cutting.

D'Alton, as we have seen, was unsympathetic to the well and to the customs associated with it and the railway company appears to have been no more concerned than he was. Indeed the minutes of the company and those of the Royal Hospital record exchanges relating to such details as watering ponds for cattle and water-pipes, but there is no minute of either party interesting itself in the fate of St John's Well.

There were, however, others who valued it more highly. The font or basin and the granite arch in which the font had stood on the old site were removed to the new catholic church in James's Street, for which the foundation stone was laid by Daniel O'Connell on 4 April 1844. There they became an ornamental feature of the garden and the arch remains at the same location. In May 1971 the font was acquired by the Knights of Malta, who set it up at 'St John's House', their new headquarters in Donnybrook.

The Knights trace their descent, albeit interrupted, from the Knights Hospitallers. At their Clyde Road premises water flows into the old font and, on ceremonial occasions, it is flood-lit.[11]

The public, moreover, were not entirely deprived of St John's Well for a new outlet was now found for the spring which had fed it. On an ordnance survey map of 1846-7 the new opening of the well is shown across the South Circular Road and up the hill, opposite Bully's Acre. Here in 1887 Wakeman sketched the arched recess which covered the fresh opening. The well was to remain accessible at this location until the turn of the century. That this new outlet was uphill and south-west of the former opening suggests that the water had always flowed thence to the former outlet, a fact which may not have been appreciated before the cutting was made and which, perhaps, explains D'Alton's location of the well as being to the south of the railway line.[12]

19 St John's Well, sketched at its new location, 1887.

In 1844 the *Dublin Gazetteer* remarked that 'the old approach [to the Royal Hospital] was through the most putrid part of the ancient city and western outlets of Dublin, but the present one is a pleasant drive'. Yet, notwithstanding the fact that four general sessions of the peace were now being held annually at Kilmainham courthouse, in addition to sittings of a local manor court, the *Dublin Gazetteer* of 1844 and Thom's *Directory* of 1850 respectively described Kilmainham as still being a 'trivial' suburb and a 'poor outlet' and considered it to be of little interest except for its antiquities. The *Gazetteer* reported that it had a population of 670. with more families employed in manufacture and trade or 'the direction of labour' than in farming.

The one place in Kilmainham which was thought to be worth visiting was the Royal Hospital and on 8 August 1849, during their brief trip to Ireland, Queen Victoria and Prince Albert deigned to call upon the old men:

> Her majesty went into some of the soldiers' rooms, and addressed the veterans in the following words: 'I am glad indeed to see you all so very comfortable'.[13]

20 Western avenue of Royal Hospital, *c.*1890,
with the wall of Bully's Acre on the left.

That her majesty's visit did not immediately bring prosperity and con-
tentment to all of those who lived in Kilmainham, may be seen from the
report of a meeting of residents in 1867. These had assembled to adopt an
Act of Parliament creating the township of New Kilmainham, which was to
include the districts of Islandbridge, Inchicore and Goldenbridge. Old Kilmainham had earlier been absorbed within the municipal and parliamentary
boundaries of the city of Dublin.

In the course of the nineteenth century a number of suburbs around
Dublin formed themselves into townships in order to address effectively the
need for adequate roads and lighting, and for clean water and sanitation in
particular. It was no doubt because of his well-known concern for sanitary
arrangements that Dr Evory Kennedy of Clondalkin was invited by the
residents in 1867 to chair their meeting. Kennedy observed that,

> There was no more neglected district, perhaps in Ireland than this, in
> the precincts of a large town. They had no sewerage, no water, no
> lighting, and no access from that of Dublin.

Dr Kennedy complained that there was an open sewer, into which was
discharged the sewage from Richmond Barracks. He added that within the
last few years they had had epidemics of cholera and fever and 'even lately
some cases of black death'.[14]

Behind the initiative to create a local township were industrialists such
as David McBirney, a prominent draper and textile producer, whose store

on the Dublin quays survived until recently. He became the first chairman of the township and continued to act in that capacity for over a decade. Less enthusiastic at first was Kilmainham's largest employer, the Great Southern and Western Railway Company, whose engineering works at Inchicore had grown to be the largest in the Dublin area and which feared a check on its freedom.[15]

In her study of Dublin in the second half of the nineteenth century, Mary E. Daly has described New Kilmainham as a 'self-contained village', in which lived just 6.3 per cent of all suburban residents around Dublin. She points out that most of its residents were either soldiers, employees of the Great Southern and Western Company engineering works or of some smaller factories, or warders at Kilmainham gaol: 'The residents were almost exclusively working class. In 1868 only sixteen houses were valued at more than £20'.[16]

By 1879 the railway company employed '1200 first-class hands at their works, of whom one third lives in the company's houses, one third in Kilmainham and one third in Dublin'. The company itself owned 148 houses at Inchicore, occupied by 850 persons. It provided no medical services for its staff and, if they were ill, these had to stay at home or go to Dublin. There was now a regular omnibus service from Inchicore to College-Green and a catholic chapel was erected at Inchicore in the 1870s.[17]

With the passing of the act creating a new township of Kilmainham in 1868, the railway company decided to participate in its administration and two of its staff were amongst those initially elected as commissioners. Daly notes that they and their colleagues made incessant efforts at Kilmainham Assizes, 'with some success', to reduce the number of licensed premises in their area. These were thought to undermine prosperity. The commissioners may have been incensed particularly by the manner in which one vintner disregarded their efforts to improve local sanitation facilities. This was Mr Woodroffe, whose nineteen cottages had just one privy between them and the overflow from this ran between two rows of cottages and ended in a stagnant pool. The officers of Islandbridge barracks held these circumstances to be responsible for recurrent epidemics of enteric fever but the law proved ineffective when Woodroffe was summoned seventeen times between 1874 and 1878.[18]

Kilmainham was not all open sewers and drunkenness at this time. The area had its pleasant side too, as one visitor later remembered. There were

> The white flowers of the *ranunculus aquaticus* [crowfoot] on the face of the stream [Camac], the wild blue succory [chicory] in the fields, the [pinkish-white] catchfly on the old walls, and the *allium vineale*, or crow-garlic [wild onion], on the adjacent banks. This, with other romantic plants, till very recently grew luxuriantly in the neighbour-

hood. People said they were survivors of the herbs which the knights
... planted to give zest to their Friday fare; and their taste and odour
could not be mistaken in the butter which was made from the
Kilmainham pastures.[19]

Into the more pastoral part of Kilmainham in 1887 came the Little Sisters of the Poor. They acquired a large cabbage field off the S. C. Rd. and
raised funds to build St Patrick's Home for the aged and poor.[20]

The township was the scene of considerable excitement during the 1880s
when supporters of the land agitation were imprisoned in Kilmainham.
There they were serenaded on St Patrick's night by a band which led a

21 Parnell arrives at Kilmainham Gaol, 1881.

throng of supporters to the gaol. Most distinguished among the arrested leaders was Charles Stewart Parnell. His incarceration brought crowds to the area as the government sought means to end a national crisis. In 1882 Parnell was freed following agreement between himself and Prime Minister Gladstone on the terms of what became known as 'the Kilmainham treaty', a document connected with the demands of the Land League.

Meanwhile, St John's Well had continued to attract visitors at its new opening, some of whom were of a more sober nature than other devotees of the place. A large Temperance meeting was convened there by Fr John Spratt (1795-1871), a Carmelite priest who was as prominent in that cause in Dublin as was Fr Theobald Mathew nationally. St John's Well was reported to have been

> the scene of true happiness on Sunday evening last. The Very Rev. Dr Spratt arrived at 5 o'clock with several other great temperance advocates, preceded by two excellent bands. A number of most useful and animating speeches were delivered, and the Very Rev. Dr Spratt administered the pledge to some thousands who returned home greatly delighted with their evening enjoyment.[21]

There were still those, however, who made their way to Kilmainham in a more traditional manner. The gatherings may not have been as festive or as popular as they used to be yet, on 25 June 1886, one witness reported that

> On the previous evening, about 9 o'clock, a strange gathering took place at the erstwhile famous well of St John of Kilmainham. Truly we are a conservative people clinging with astonishing faith to old world habits and to ancient customs ... despite all these things [proclamations etc.] on St John's Eve 1886 there go forth from the heart of the Liberties some hundreds of the poor who congregate round the place forgotten by all save themselves. Near the well a detachment of police are stationed, for the curious assemblages are not always orderly.[22]

Ten years later the days of the well at its new opening were finally numbered by a writer in the *Irish Builder*. Describing the arch on the west side of S. C. Rd. as being 'rather what represents the form of a well' this witness forecast that

> In the course of a few years hence all trace of St John's Well will be lost, as we understand that a new range of buildings (artisan's dwellings) are now nearly completed, which when finished, the wall on

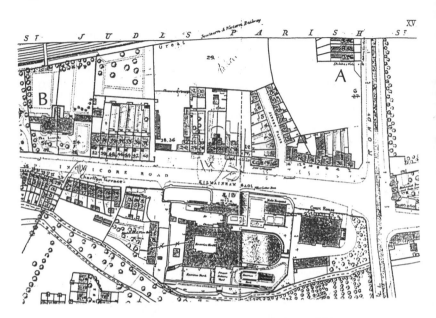

22 (*above*) Valuation Office map 1902 marked 'A' and 'B'.
(*below left*) Area marked 'B' enlarged and showing the location of a spring recently
discovered at '2. The Laurels', also known as 'Kilmainham Well House';
(*below right*) Area marked 'A' enlarged, showing location of St John's Well *c.*1845-1902.

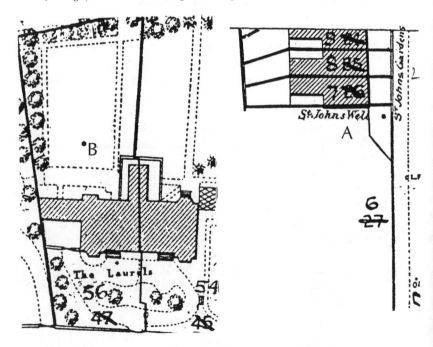

the west side will be taken down, and all trace of this once famous well will finally disappear.[23]

The railway and the expansion of the city were bringing new inhabitants to the area in growing numbers. By 1896 Thom's *Directory* was giving the population of the township as no less than 6516. This increase was creating a demand for new housing in the district and during the last decade of the century the short terrace known as St John's Gardens (the 'artisan's dwellings' to which the *Irish Builder* had referred), was erected across the road from Bully's Acre. A map of 1902 indicates that the terrace began immediately north of the arched recess containing the opening of St John's Well – but a map of 1907 shows no sign of the well. Shortly afterwards Joyce wrote that the well remained at the niche until it was, 'a few years ago...ruthlessly swept away during the alterations consequent upon the building of St John's [Gardens]'.

> Even up to the time of its disappearance, the well was not without a few old pilgrims on St John's Day, some for devotional purposes, and others to procure some of the water, which on the anniversary was believed to possess a peculiar sanctity.

St John Joyce stated that 'a flat slab of stone in the waste plot adjoining St John's [Gardens] appears to mark the recent site of this ancient well, which it is presumed has met the ignoble fate of being drained into the street sewer'. It is a tantalising possibility that this slab was an ancient slab from the well.[24]

A single undated plan of the layout of St John's Gardens, which for no obvious reason is in the National Library, shows no sign of the well and gives the lane as having footpaths, which suggests that it may have been intended to use it as an access for further housing backing onto the railway. More recently the lane was closed by a gate.[25]

The twentieth century

In August 1900 the Dublin Boundaries Bill became law and Kilmainham, along with the townships of Drumcondra and Clontarf, was absorbed into the city of Dublin. This was a measure which for over twenty years had been sought by the corporation. The city had a disproportionate number of working class citizens and suffered from major housing and social problems. As the middle class moved out to new suburbs during the nineteenth century, Dublin Corporation lost revenue and became increasingly eager to extend its boundaries. Between 1879 and 1881 an attempt to absorb Kilmainham, Drumcondra, Pembroke and Rathmines had been foiled by prominent people who lived there. This was notwithstanding the fact that there was not a main sewer in the entire township of Kilmainham and that there was 'not any real staff to carry out the work of the township'. However, by the end of the century, Dublin's needs were such that the expansion of the city's boundaries proved irresistible.[1]

The inmates of the Royal Hospital may have followed these developments with some interest for, if a picture published in 1900 is indicative, they were very keen readers. It shows some of the 'old men' gathered in a room, individually perusing a wide range of publications. This image no doubt heartened those who needed to be reassured not only that public money was being spent appropriately on the army but that the pensioners appreciated their good fortune. For there were some who were sceptical of the need to maintain such an elaborate institution, which seemed to be regarded by soldiers as a place of last-resort. As we saw above, the possibility that it might close had been raised and defeated in the 1830s. It recurred, with some critics suspecting that the premises were enjoyed more by those currently serving in the upper echelons of the army than by mere pensioners. Thus, in 1851, the secretary for war, Fox Maule MP, thought that

> Kilmainham was rather kept up for show than use, many officers of
> high rank having chambers there, and but a small part of the build-
> ing being appropriated to its original object.

Maule defended himself against suggestions that an instruction to the commander to admit no more pensioners was a ploy to close the Royal Hospital and explained hastily that he merely wanted more careful scrutiny of applications. As the government backed off in the face of opposition the institution survived although, as we have already observed, the number of pensioners on its 'establishment' was reduced.[2]

23 'After many battles'. Old men at the Royal Hospital, 1900.

There is no doubt that the value of the place to the army was partly social. Great balls and other events took place in the hall and in 1893 a magazine for ladies considered it worth their while to publish a feature on the elegant circumstances in which the daughter of the commander then lived at Kilmainham.[3]

In the first decade of the twentieth century it was suggested by Lord MacDonald and others that the buildings and grounds of the Royal Hospital might be put to better use as a campus of the new National University of Ireland, founded in 1908. As we now know, however, it was ultimately decided instead to house University College Dublin at Earlsfort Terrace. Students of U.C.D. and Trinity College Dublin did resort to the area in order to boat on the Liffey.[4]

That the Royal Hospital might yet prove to have a value to the army in times of crisis was underlined during the Easter Rebellion of 1916, when 2500 troops were slung into its defence. These came under fire from insurgents who occupied the Malt House in Bow Lane but two-machine gun sections took up position on a roof within the grounds of the hospital and silenced the attackers. The national leaders of the Rebellion were subsequently arrested and, along were many of their followers, interned in the Richmond Barracks. Then, in notorious circumstances, most of those leaders were executed at Kilmainham Gaol. As the volleys echoed around the neighbourhood there can have been few who anticipated that much of Ireland would become a free state within five years. The gaol was still in use during the War of Independence and during the Civil War, when four soldiers of the anti-treaty side were executed on 17 November 1922. In 1924 the last of the Republican prisoners was released from Kilmainham. No longer used for holding prisoners, the building lay idle for many years but a campaign from the 1960s onwards led to its being partly renovated and reopened for visitors. It is believed to be haunted.[5]

On 17 December 1922 the commander-in-chief of the British Army bade farewell to Kilmainham. The Royal Hospital had become the last post of the British Army in 'Southern Ireland' and it was now handed over to the forces of the new government. There were some mild protests when the celebrated old armoury was carted off to England with the departing soldiers. Most of this had only come to Kilmainham in 1891, much of it in the first place being imported from London some decades earlier, but the collection did include the ornamental swords carried by the yeomen of the guard of the Irish houses of parliament. These were said to date from the seventeenth century. Some pensioners remained behind in residence at the Royal Hospital.[6]

It was not long before the new government was considering to what use it might put the premises of the Royal Hospital and in July 1923, just two

24 University Boat Club and Inchicore Road, *c.*1890.

months after the end of the Civil War, President Cosgrave announced that
plans were available for the adaptation of the Royal Hospital as the future
home of the Oireachtas. The proposal, which had been under consideration since at least January, was that the lower house would meet in the great
hall and that the upper house would sit in the chapel. A committee of
members was appointed to consider the matter.[7]

The intention at the time was to create a suitable permanent home for
the new parliament, as Leinster House was considered to be too cramped
and it was thought that the Royal Hospital could be altered as needed
without excessive expenditure. There was also space on which to erect new
offices and the prospect of various improvements to the area prompted the
correspondent of the *Manchester Guardian* to proclaim:

> If these buildings are given the honour, it will be interesting to see
> how the western side of the capital will be affected. The main road
> to parliament would at first be one of the oldest, most interesting and
> most lamentably squalid in Dublin. The whole area on the city side
> of the Royal Hospital is astonishingly eighteenth-century, but only
> painters and students of door-posts would much regret its disappear-
> ance.[8]

One correspondent to the *Irish Times* informed its readers that Provost
Mahaffy of Trinity College had some years earlier expressed the view that
the Royal Hospital would indeed be an appropriate home for an Irish parliament. However, the editor of the *Evening Telegraph* was not alone is ques-
tioning the convenience of the site.[9] Dublin was still a compact metropolis
and its main institutions were within easy walking distance of each other.
Others were unhappy about the historical associations of the place with the
British. In any event the plan was dropped.

In the history of the Royal Hospital published in 1921 it was said that

> a superstition hangs about the place to the effect that if the rooks
> which build [their nests] in the main avenue leave it, fortune for a
> time leaves the Hospital. About 1916 the rook took their departure,
> and only returned in 1921.[10]

In 1927 the birds may have gone again when the last of the pensioners
departed, for the property then went into decline. It served for some years as
the headquarters of the Gardai but, in 1949, they too abandoned it and the
buildings were subsequently used as stores by the National Museum. The
great trees, which Lawrence had photographed and which the rooks enjoyed, were themselves felled. Not until the 1980s would the old Royal
Hospital find a new lease of life and today, on the western avenue, young

25 Enjoying the Irish Museum of Modern Art.

trees grow taller every year and people come to view the exhibitions of the Irish Museum of Modern Art.

The Free State government did decide to make official use of the old court-house at Kilmainham, much to the chagrin of lawyers and merchants who had been only too happy to see it closed in 1911 and business moved to Green street. The fact that the legal profession also thought that Kilmainham was an inconvenient location did not deter the state from re-opening its court-house for the transaction of County Dublin civil cases. Thus, from October 1924, the old sessions-house became part of the new district court system and criminal cases also came in due course to be heard there.[11]

Another controversial decision which the new government made was to allow the disposal of the old Richmond Barracks for public housing. Earlier the military institution had been renamed 'Keogh Barracks' after Tom Keogh, a Dublin guard killed in a mine explosion near Macroom in the early days of the Civil War. As 'Keogh Square', the converted buildings earned a reputation as one of the worst slums in the Republic of Ireland.[12]

SURVIVAL OF THE WELL?

If St John's Well has not been visible since the beginning of the twentieth century, the spring or springs which fed it have not dried up. Indeed, one of the characteristic legends concerning holy wells is similar to that which we associated earlier with sacred fires, namely that they have managed to preserve themselves or be preserved against various attempts to spoil or to block them: 'straightaway the well dries up and breaks out somewhere else, usually nearby but sometimes a mile or more away or on the other side of a river'.[13]

And in this effort at preservation they have not only had the encouragement of popular custom or superstition but also the sympathy of some learned individuals.

As we have seen, there is a long history of writers from outside the Gaelic tradition scoffing at and disapproving of the folklore and practices associated with holy wells. In the twelfth century Giraldus Cambrensis was already describing a 'barbarous rite, without rime or reason', which was associated with a well in Munster.[14] A number of more recent and more caustic observations on the subject have been included earlier. It has also been seen that the native Irish too, including some like Archbishop Carpenter who shared in the learned Gaelic tradition, became embarrassed by and ashamed of the rituals, drunkenness, violence and licence associated with many gatherings at holy wells.

As early as the Synod of Armagh in 1614 and the Synod of Tuam in 1660 the bishops had issued strictures to discourage 'revelling, junketing, profane pipe and flute playing, dancing and boisterous behaviour' at such sites and later members of the hierarchy echoed their concerns.[15] What was perceived to be a degeneration in the custom compromised those who were seeking to roll back the penal laws and those who subsequently attempted to build a new Ireland on the basis of opportunities provided by Catholic Emancipation.

However, there have always been people who saw something worthwhile in the tradition of paying homage at holy wells. In 1662, in a riposte to travel writers such as Giraldus, John Lynch observed: 'travellers (says our Irish proverb) bring home a patent for lying'. And as recently as 1926 John Neary wrote in the *Irish Ecclesiastical Review*:

> After the Great Famine alien clerics came tip-toeing and capering throughout the West, and assuming a high moral tone, poured obloquy and derision on the unaffected devotion that centred around the wells. Throw enough dirt and some will stick.[16]

During the twentieth century the focus of popular devotion has been centred on Marian statues rather than on holy wells. For example, it is said that within the space of two years from its erection in the 1930s, a grotto at the back of the Church of Mary Immaculate on Tyrconnell Road, Inchicore, attracted one million visitors. The grotto was known popularly as 'the Irish Lourdes'.[17] More recently, in rural Ireland, crowds have flocked to see 'moving statues'. Few now gather at the simple holy springs.

Many who drive past the old wells today find nothing to be gained from revisiting the past. Yet, others are increasingly perturbed by what they perceive to be a process of cultural homogenisation and by disrespect for the environment. There is a fresh appreciation of ancient traditions.

There are, or used to be, 3000 or more holy wells in Ireland. Kelly's casual aside of 1848 that St John's Well, Meath, was 'a beautiful spring' and a very recent mention of the 'beautiful azure blue pool, scarcely six inches across,' which is the very ancient 'Tooth Well' on the Burren in Co. Clare, are just two intimations of the kind of wonder which people felt when they gazed down through clear calm water at the nourishment bubbling up below and then flowing away across their earth.[18]

Generation after generation came to the same sources of wonder and healing. Cures might be sought and sometimes granted, but the expression of faith was undiminished. At a number of sites some element of respect and attention may still be found. The fact that devotions are again celebrated at St John's Well in County Meath suggests that Christians may find something more at such places than the faint traces of sacrificial ceremonies which would be utterly unacceptable to any contemporary religious sensitivity. Indeed, in 1995 the Irish catholic bishops publicly defined penitential pilgrimages to local holy wells as 'characteristic' of Irish catholicism.[19]

St John Joyce feared that the water of St John at Kilmainham had been lost forever in some Dublin sewer, but is it necessarily so? In the nineteenth century the local well survived the coming of the railways when a new outflow was opened for it, south and west of its earlier location. Then this was lost in the building of St John's Gardens. In 1958 Kevin Danaher went looking for some sign of St John's Well and found that 'an iron hatch-cover on the west side of Islandbridge Road, opposite Bully's Acre, seems to mark the site of this once famous well'. There is no trace of this well now between St John's Gardens and the ground at the back of the adjacent Rowntree Nestlé chocolate factory.[20]

There are certainly a number of other springs or wells in the area, as may be seen from an inspection of successive ordnance survey maps. About 1818 one visitor to Kilmainham made no specific reference to St John's Well but did note that, at the Royal Hospital, 'the ground has, indeed, several springs, and in one of the vaults is a well producing water of an excellent quality, but this not fit for washing or culinary purposes'. In 1948, as we shall see in the epilogue, Bersu discovered a medieval well near Bully's Acre. Indeed, during the period when the present history was being written by this author, a fresh outflow of clear water was opened in the rear garden of the aptly-named Kilmainham Well House. It is a short distance from where St John's Well was last seen. And where St John's Well was long associated with the founding abbot of the monastery of Kilmainham, this most recent spring was in 1994 divined by the founding abbot of another monastery.[21]

Epilogue

During 1995 the National Museum mounted an exhibition entitled 'Viking Age Ireland', thereby drawing attention to the significance of Kilmainham and to its existence as a settlement as old and older than Dublin. However, at present there appears to be no prospect of any major archaeological dig being undertaken in the area and such Viking remains as have been found have been discovered largely by chance in the course of excavations for the roads and railway and in the creation of the Memorial Park at Island-bridge.

Fortunately, much of the Kilmainham area is not built upon, including the Royal Hospital grounds, the eastern side of Rowntree Nestlé's property and the park. A systematic examination of these lands might yield very significant results. Not only Viking remains but also signs of pre-Viking monastic activity and of the later knights may remain to be discovered, particularly in Bully's Acre and in the grassy acres or 'hospital fields' between Bully's Acre and the main Royal Hospital building. This building now houses the Irish Museum of Modern Art. In 1921 Childers and Stewart observed:

> There is a hollow in the Master's Fields to the west of the present house, along the crescent of which the ancient buildings ran. The eye may follow what appear to be the traces of foundations.[1]

In 1948 Gerhard Bersu, a German archaeologist who had been interned on the Isle of Man during World War II, carried out some excavations at the Royal Hospital. From his notebooks in the National Museum he appears to have made a number of cuttings in the same area as that to which Childers and Stewart referred and to have found in the direction of Bully's Acre pavement slabs, an old well and a stone wall. He also discovered fragments of medieval tiles, including one of a line-impressed lion rampant which is unusual in that the beast is shown facing left. Unfortunately, the location of the well and slabs is not now visible. We saw in earlier chapters suggestions by McNeill and others that there was once a tiled floor, possibly of a church, in the vicinity of the granite shaft in Bully's Acre.[2]

The restoration and development of the old Royal Hospital in recent years has, justifiably, been widely welcomed but the manner of its execution has, at times, been controversial. Before any further development takes place which might disturb the soil between the museum proper and Bully's Acre, there may be much to gain both for the museum and for the public

from exploring the uneven levels
of this area in order to discover if
they conceal the foundations of the
castle and priory of the knights.
Modern scanning techniques could
be employed in conjunction with
more conventional methods of
investigation.[3]

In 1981 human remains were
found under the western avenue
and placed in a hole in Bully's
Acre. Also in recent years the old
granite shaft was knocked down,
apparently by a mechanical digger.
The impact fractured the monument into three pieces, which have
been stuck back together, as may be
seen clearly by any visitor who
inspects it.[4] This is an important
and forgotten stone which could in
time come to be recognised by the
public as a feature of Kilmainham
and to attract visitors to the Museum.

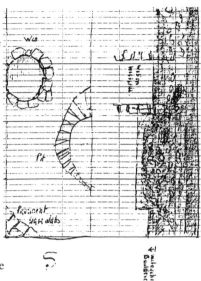

27 Sketch by Bersu of limited archaeological
excavations at Royal Hospital, 1948,
showing well, pit and pavement.

The old cemetery of Bully's Acre is overgrown at present and would
benefit from greater attention. The wall around it is broken and it is not
difficult to enter within. Hidden in the bushes are pieces of an old imperial
monument, including at least one charming cherub. In a corner of the
enclosure the level of the floor of a large old brick shed is considerably
below that in the rest of the walled area and this may suggest that much of
the present top-soil was only laid on the cemetery when the Circular Road
was built. If so, this layer may have acted to protect the original level from
excessive digging during the later cholera epidemic. During the recent wid-
ening of St John's Road West and South Circular Road to meet the new
Chapelizod by-pass, a limited dig revealed the remains of a passageway from
the area of St John's Well towards Bully's Acre and of what seems to have
been a gate-lodge, perhaps that 'House of St John's Well' mentioned by
Trail in his report of 1795.[5]

The earth of Kilmainham may yet yield some important finds, relating
not only to the Viking age but also to our Gaelic and Anglo-Norman past.
Any development plan for the area ought to refer not only to the legacy of
these earlier eras but also to the preservation and utilisation of relics of the
more recent industrial and urban past. In this respect the recent construction of a museum at Kilmainham Gaol is a milestone.

Appendix A: Name and Genealogy of Maignenn

In relation both to genealogical details and to the translation of the passage from Colgan below, the assistance of Dr Máirín Ní Dhonnchadha of the School of Celtic Studies, Dublin Institute for Advanced Studies, is gratefully acknowledged.

The saint's name is found spelt in a number of ways. That adopted here is 'Maignenn'. Also found are 'Maigind', 'Magnenn', 'Ma[i]gnend[us]', 'Maighneen', 'Maigne' or 'Ma[i]gni[u/n]', etc. It is common to have variant spellings of the names of saints. It is possible too for a saint to be remembered more than once each year and Saint Maignenn was celebrated not only on 18 December but also on 19 October. Most sources identify both dates as being devoted to the same man but it may be that there were two saints of the same name, especially given the familial nature of offices in the early church. There was also a St Mainchin of Kilmanihin.[1]

Basic information about the ancestry of Maignenn is contained in the accounts of his life which are in London and Paris (see Appendix B). These agree that 'Maignenn, and Toa, and Librén, and Cobthach, were the four sons of Áedh', who was son of Colgan son of Tuathal son of Felim son of Colla fó Chríth (also Colla fo chrich/Colla-dá-Chrích).

In the mid-seventeenth century Colgan added to our store of information. Trawling through manuscripts, some of which are no longer extant, he wrote in his *magnum opus* that Librén

> and three additional brothers are listed in the Catalogue of Saints, that is S. Maignenn abbot of Cill Maignenn in close proximity to Dublin, S. Cobthach, and S. Tuan [Toa], said to have been the sons of Áed son of Colcu, of the house of Airgialla in [the territory of the] Ulaid. Here, however, Librén son of Áed is seen to have lived close to the beginning of the seventh century, for his father Áed died in the year 606 according to the native annals where at that year we read concerning him: 'Áed son of Colcu, lord of Airgialla, died'.[2]

Colgan gives 1 April as the feast day of Tuan but O'Hanlon notes that little is known of this saint, whom some say had lived for 1500 years up to the time of St Patrick! The descendants of the legendary Colla fo Críth, the Airthir and Uí Chremthainn, were located in an area extending over the modern counties of Armagh and parts of Monaghan and Fermanagh.[3]

The author of the 'Martyrology of Donegal' also states that Maignenn was 'of the race' of Colla fó Chríth. This source adds that 'Senell, daughter of Cenannan, sister of Old Senchell the saint, was his mother'.[4]

This 'Old Senchell' (also known as Senshinchell/Senshinell/ Sinchell sen/Sinell Sen/Senchell Sen/Senshenchell /Sincheall) is reputed by some sources to have been 330 years old when he died, although a more conservative estimate gives 130 as his age at death! A former disciple of Saint Patrick, he was abbot of a monastery at Killeagh, near Tullamore, Co. Offaly, when he passed away about AD 550. Earlier he had occupied the church of 'Cluain-Damh', an uncertain location perhaps in or near the lower Liffey valley where there was a striking concentration of early monastic sites. This church is said to have been given to him by St Ailbe[us], who was one of the earliest missionaries to Ireland and a contemporary of Patrick. At least one source gives Ailbe's age at death as 140.[5]

Dr Ní Dhonnchadha writes that it is not possible from the genealogy of Maignenn 'to hazard a *floruit* for him, as none of the individuals in his genealogy has a precise date, and his remote so-called ancestor, Colla fó Chríth, is a legendary figure. In any case, his genealogy looks suspiciously short. His descent on the maternal side is equally unhelpful, as again the individuals named cannot be dated, as far as I know'.[6]

MacCana has pointed out how St Brighid 'usurped' the role of the goddess who was her namesake and there are similar examples of transference in the case of other early saints. One may speculate that the figure and celebration of Maignenn absorbed certain characteristics of an earlier figure such as Manannan but there is no firm evidence to support such a notion. There was a pre-Christian cult of Manannan Mac Lir, the Celtic God of the sea, and on the Isle of Man, which was named after him, he was sometimes celebrated at midsummer.[7]

Appendix B: Manuscript accounts of Maignenn

There are known to be two extant medieval accounts of Saint Maignenn, both in Irish but neither kept in Ireland. In London there is the 'Account of the sayings and doings of Saint Magniu or Maignenn of Kilmainham, Co. Dublin' and in Paris there is 'Betha Maignenn'.[1]

Todd, Omont and Kenney provide minimal information on the content of the Paris manuscript, of which there is a weak microfilm copy in the National Library of Ireland. However, I obtained a copy of the manuscript from Paris and Dr Máirín Ní Dhonnchadha very kindly compared this for me with O'Grady's transcript of the London manuscript which was published in the nineteenth century.[2]

As regards the relationship between the the published version of the homiletic text on Maignenn which is in London and the Paris manuscript, Dr Ní Dhonnchadha writes that:

> both versions are substantially the same (differences in wording and spelling are minimal);
> both versions appear to have been written by the same scribe;
> both versions are incomplete, and break off at the same point. This suggests either that both derive from a common exemplar, or that one derives from the other.

This author has himself visited the British Library to inspect its 'Account' of Maignenn. It appears to have been quite fairly copied and translated by O'Grady. Certainly O'Grady has included the text from opening to close, although he may have somewhat enhanced the original where the usual manuscript contractions make it particularly terse.[3]

Precise transcriptions and annotated translations of the Paris and London manuscripts would be welcome. Sharpe does not mention Maignenn in his major study of the accounts in Latin of Irish saints and he tells this author in a letter that he knows nothing of the saint. This underlines the fact that the only known accounts are in the vernacular.[4]

The London and Paris manuscripts are thought to have been transcribed or written down in the fifteenth century by one Uilliam Mac an Leagha (William MacAlea), a member of a family of hereditary physicians. There are believed to be two other manuscripts from the 1460s by the same person. In the Students' Reading Room of the British Library a typed catalogue of the Egerton collection states that the account of Maignenn is 'ascribed to the xii century', but this appears to be an error.[5]

On the first folio of Egerton MS 91 a later hand has written 'The Leabhar Breach: old lives of ancient Irish saints, &c in the Irish language: valuable manuscript'. The text is different from that 'Leabhar Breach' which has been published in facsimile and which, apart from anything else, lacks a life of Maignenn. Another hand has scribbled headings on particular folios of Egerton MS 91 to indicate the contents thus:

> Paul, Abraham. Colmcille. Brendan [?-looks like ben Find]. Gregory. Hell & Divinity. Heaven. Bishops of the church. Ciaran. Martin or a martyr. John the Baptist. Maineng [corrected to 'Maingend' but the MS text gives 'Maigind']. Seanan. The Druid baptised. Brigid. Egyptian monks. Wonderful Parnut(ius) abbot etc. Early martyrs. Jesus. Roman Empire.

As regards Colmcille a later gloss notes, 'exceedingly ancient in style. It is of Cc [Colmcille], mentions kings before Christ, mentions patriarch Ciaran and calls the bishop of Rome a "high bishop"'. Another gloss has 'I have proved this all right (1823)'!

A reference to Maignenn is also found in accounts of the life of Fursa, a saint of the seventh century. They tell how the two men exchanged their diseases in token of friendship.[6] Ó hOgain regards this story as a local variant of the international folktale which tells of how a snake enters a person's stomach and is enticed out again by being made thirsty. He adds that later, when Fursa was abroad, a bishop censured him for his voraciousness, whereupon the saint caused the disease or 'reptile' of Maignenn to enter the bishop's throat. The bishop then understood and Fursa recalled the reptile to himself.[7]

O'Hanlon indicates that Fursa was a highly respected Irish monk who died about AD 650, having left Ireland a quarter of a century earlier to preach in England and to become abbot of Lagny in France.[8] His meeting with Maignenn occurred in the early seventh century, perhaps.

Appendix C: Wise man, healer or philosopher of Kilmainham?

As seen above in chapter 3, Lerghus Ua Fidhchain is said to have died at Kilmainham in the 780s. His passing was noted by the old Irish annalists whose records have come down to us largely through later transcriptions

The most ancient of the extant manuscripts which refer to Lerghus is more than five hundred years old and it, like most of the handful of relevant manuscripts, describes him as 'a sage' or 'wise-man'. Indeed Maignenn too has been described in the 'Account' as a 'sage' and it may be significant that the 'orthodox' etymology of the word 'druid' gives 'very wise man'.[1]

However, there is at least one indication that another epithet was also used to describe Learghus, namely 'iccnaidh'. This word does not appear in the *Dict. Ir. Lang.* and the closest word to it which is given is 'iccaidh', which means both a 'healer' and one who pays or suffers. There were two kinds of Gaelic doctor, the 'liaig' and the 'iccaidh'. The latter was almost literally a faith-healer. Says Davies of the word 'iccaidh': 'its curative connotation had to do with the benefits of general care, rather than the administering of medicine ... with preservation from death and with salvation rather than with medicinal remedies'. Herbal remedies do not appear to have had a big place in Gaelic medicine.[2]

The relevant extant references which I have located are:

Before 1498
Annals of Ulster (T.C.D. MS). An old vellum manuscript in Latin, giving at f.34v 'Lerghus nepos Fidhcain sapiens chille Maighninn'. *Annals of Ulster,* ed. Hennessy, gives 'Lerghus Ua Fidhcain, a wise man of Cill-Maighnenn'. Recently *Annals of Ulster*, ed. MacAirt and MacNiocaill, p. 242 translates it as 'the learned Lergus grandson of Fidchain of Cell Maignenn'. Hennessy (iv, p. viii) states that this part of the manuscript was written by Cathal MacManus, Dean of Lough Erne. MacManus died in 1498. Although 'chastity' was one of the characteristics attributed to MacManus, he is also said to have fathered two sons and is described as a 'concubinary'.

About 1627
Annals of Clonmacnoise (T.C.D. MS; British Library MS); *Annals of Clonmacnoise,* p.126: These are in English, all from a lost original, and give only 'Lergus O'ffiachayn the sage of Kellmaynam'.

Later 1600s

Annals in Irish from the year 457 (Brit. Lib. MS). These annals, apparently
a seventeenth century transcription, are in confused chronological order
and I could find no entry for the 780s.

1734-5

A transcription made AD 1734-5 by Hugh O'Molloy, of annals in Irish
(T.C.D. MS). This has 'Leargus Ua Fidhchain, eagn cille maighnin'. 'Eagn'
is probably a contraction of 'eagnach', meaning 'a wise-man' or 'sage'.
O'Donovan has described O'Molloy as an 'excellent and well-qualified
scribe' but notes that he was bad at contractions (*AFM*, p. viii, p. xxxii).
We do not know if 'eagn' is an exact copy of an older contraction or a stab
at rendering an older contraction in some meaningful way.

About 1764

A transcription of annals in Irish made *c*. AD 1764, perhaps by Maurice
O'Gorman (T.C.D. MS). Gives 'Leargus Ua Fidhchain, iccnaidh cille
maigneann'. 'Iccnaidh' with an 'n' may be a misreading of 'eagn' or 'ecn'
for 'eagnach' or 'ecnach'.

1826

O'Connor, *Rerum Hibernicarum Scriptores*,, iii, apparently viewing the same
manuscript as O'Molloy (above), has 'Leargus Ua Fidhchain, eccn, cille
Maignenn' and offers in Latin 'sapiens' for 'eccn', taking it to be 'ecnach'.

1856

In the standard version of the old annals, translated and published by
O'Donovan (*AFM*), the editor hedges his bets. Without any explanation or
footnote he gives 'iccnaidh' in the Irish text and 'wise-man' in the English'.

It must be said, from the evidence available, that 'wise-man' or 'sage' is
more likely than 'healer' to have been the epithet originally applied to
Lerghus. Some writers on Dublin have described him as a 'philosopher'.[3]
The word 'philosopher', with its connotation of the study of Plato, is mis-
leading. If the reputed wisdom of Lerghus was more than pure insight then
it possibly referred to skill in biblical exegesis.[4]

A fifteenth-century manuscript in London refers to Kilmainham in the
context of a consideration of scientific experiments and recipes. and culinary matters. This substantial document awaits transcription and translation
and it is not possible at present to say if it throws light on this earlier period.[5]

Notes

FOREWORD

1 For the name and feast day of Maignenn see Appedix A.
2 For old manuscript accounts of Maignenn see Appendix B.

1: AN ACCOUNT OF SAINT MAIGNENN

1 For a discussion of relevant genealogical sources see Appendix A.
2 Appendix A, n.1 for martyrologies; *Obits and Martyrology of Christ Church*, p. xlvi; Sharpe, 'Problems concerning the organisation of the church', pp. 230-70; Gwynn, 'Bishops of Dublin'; Gwynn, *The Irish church*, p. 64.
3 Sharpe, 'Quatuor sanctissimi episcopi', p. 385; Ryan, *Irish monasticism*, p. 117.
4 Flower, *Catalogue*, ii, 446; Kenney, *Sources*, p. 466. For the monastic context in which Maignenn lived, see Ryan, *Irish monasticism, passim*.
5 *Martyrology of Donegal*, pp. 317-18; Ryan, *Irish monasticism*, pp. 399-401, 408.
6 McNamara, 'Psalter study', pp. 206-13. The National Museum of Ireland has a set of waxed tablets from Antrim. The references in the 'Account' to leaving a 'passage free' and to 'deception' are redolent of Eastern teaching on 'chakras' and illusion. For Ciaran's fox see Stokes, *Lives of the saints*, p. 26, p. 121.
7 The text quoted here is Stokes's own translation of the passage given by him at *Martyrology of Oengus*, p. 45, but 'worm' would be a more usual translation than 'reptile', according to *Dict. Ir. lang.* For more on this story see Appendix B.
8 The twelve listed do not correspond to those listed at Ryan, *Irish monasticism*, p. 118 or those whom the late Tomás Ó Fiaich had in mind at Moody and Martin, *Course of Irish History*, p. 67.
9 Also translated at O'Curry, *Manners and customs*, p. ccxl who dates the encounter AD 538 to 558. Dermot was king of Tara, the Ui Neill over-kingship. He died in 565. Yet O'Hanlon, *Lives*, ii (7 February) says that Loman was active in the early seventh century. O'Curry uses this passage to demonstrate the existence of the 'Faine Maigdene' or 'maiden's-ring' – a tribute due to the king on the marriage of every maiden within his territory. Clearly Maignenn was not adverse to accepting valuable donations, although elsewhere in the 'Account' he is said never to have accepted either gold or silver or any metal that is denominated 'moneta'. Since 'money' as such is not thought to have been in use as currency in Ireland until the tenth century this observation may have reflected the writer's yearning for days long gone when a communal system of barter still existed. Such anachronisms as those indicated here are common in the 'Lives' of Irish saints.
10 O'Hanlon, *Lives*, ix (10 Sept. *d*.572-9).
11 Healy, 'The monastic school of St Enda of Aran', pp. 163-87 says that of all the sixth century saints 'hardly one did not spend some time on Aran'.

12 O'Hanlon, *Lives*, vi (17 June. Bishop of Ferns, *d.*696-7). The only *Bearna na
    Gaoithe* given in Hogan, *Onomasticon*, is Windgate[s] on the back of Bray Head,
    Co. Wicklow. There was once a 'Giant's Grave' at this spot. Even the location
    of this cairn is now forgotten. It was not on a direct route to Carlow from
    Kilmainham but Maignenn may have gone via Rathdown and Glendalough
    (Ware, 'Antiquities', ii, p. 202; Letter from Eugene Curry, 27 Dec. 1838, in
    Ordnance survey letters, 1839 (National Library MS), pp. 28-9, 36; Price, *Wick-
    low, v*, pp. 326-7).

13 Mochu[d/t]a, abbot of Rahan, near Tullamore, *d.*637. This area of the present
    Co. Offaly was known as 'the territory of the men of the churches' (O'Donovan,
    Book of rights, p. 179n). Meyer, *Triads of Ireland*, p. ix for 'one of three worst
    counsels to be acted upon in Ireland', namely 'the expulsion of Mochuta from
    Rathe[e]n'. For this see Kenney, *Sources*, pp. 451-2. For his 'exalted burial in
    Raithin' see text below. In medieval Ireland some regarded women as being by
    nature one third more passionate than men (O'Dwyer, *Céli Dé*, p. 105).

14 O'Hanlon, *Lives*, vii (7 July), pp. 103-5; Gwynn and Purton, 'The monastery of
    Tallaght', p. 133, p. 141 (Maelruain disapproves of excessive rigour); O'Dwyer,
    Céli Dé, passim; For 'ordeal' in hot or cold water, or fire, see Ware, *Antiquities*,
    ch. 19. Maelruain founded his church 769, *d.*789/92.

15 'Sepulture' is the act of placing in a sepulchre or tomb. For 'the correct legend'
    of this saint see Bryce, *Geology of Clydesdale*, pp. 140-1. The cave of the saint is
    still pointed out and, nearby, a holy well and a large 'judgement stone' con-
    tinue to draw pilgrims. The name of the village of Lamlash on Arran, from
    which boats sail to Holy Island, is from this saint's name and the island itself is
    known locally as 'Eilean Molaise'. O'Hanlon, *Lives*, vi (18 April) distinguishes
    between this saint and others of the same name, including a Molaise of
    Inishmurray. Pochin Mould, *The Irish saints*, pp. 203-4 notes that the saint is
    celebrated on the Scottish island on his feast day. *The Holy Island Project Newslet-
    ter 1993* (Scotland), *passim*, reports that on 18 April 1992, the feastday of Molaise,
    an order of monks and nuns from Tibet acquired Holy Island as an inter-faith
    retreat centre. This lineage is represented in Dublin by the Samyedzong Bud-
    dhist Centre at 'Kilmainham Well House'. For the dispute over Easter see
    Hughes, *The Church in early Irish society*, pp. 103-10.

16 O'Curry, *Lectures on manuscript materials*, pp. 404-6, 423-30, notes that 'the fatal
    day of St John the Baptist' was not the midsummer feast of his nativity on 24
    June but that of his beheading ('decollation') on 29 August. He describes the
    'Broom out of Fanait' as a fiery dragon and also associates this with St John
    Baptist; O'Rahilly, *Early Irish history*, pp. 520-2.

2: THE MYSTERIOUS FIRE OF KILMAINHAM.

1 O'Rahilly, *Early Irish history*, p. 172; Stokes, *Book of Lismore*, p. 156. The Patrick
   legend itself echoes an earlier conflict between Midhe and the druids (Woods,
   Annals of Westmeath, p. 241).

2 Wakeman, 'Inis Muiredach', pp. 174-332; Heraughty; *Inishmurray*, pp. 21-3, p.
   89. Both authors include illustrations.

3 Stokes, *Book of Lismore* , p. 277, p. 358; *Martyrology of Donegal*, p. 65, p. 170;

O'Hanlon, *Lives*, viii (11 August); MacNeill, *The festival of Lughnasa*, p. 406, 579-82.

4 Ware, *History and antiquities of Ireland*, p. 45; O'Meara *Topography of Ireland by Cambrensis*, pp. 81-2, 88. Topography of Ireland by Cambrensis (Nat. Lib. MS) for the sketch of the archer reproduced here, which is thought to be AD 1438 at the latest.

5 Ware, *Antiquities of Ireland*. The English text here, which I have checked against the Latin of 1654 for accuracy, is that which appeared in Dublin in 1705 (p. 45). Later editions of Ware were 'revised and improved' and changed by Walter Harris.

6 *Martyrology of Oengus*; *Martyrology of Tallaght*, sub 26 Oct. (cl.364f). MacCana, *Celtic mythology*, p. 131 writes: 'In several localities the memory remains of three holy sisters who cannot easily be dissociated from the trio of goddesses who figure so often and so prominently in the early mythological legends'.

7 Kendrick, *The Druids*, pp. 83-4, p. 87; O'Dwyer, *Céli Dé*, p. 105. For an Irish trace of animal sacrifice into modern times see MacNeill, *Lughnasa*, pp. 582-4.

8 Stokes (ed.), *Three Irish glossaries*, p. xxxv and p. 6; Anon., 'Fires of bone', p. 77; ibid., viii (1860), p. 76; Anon., 'Bonfires of St John', p. 147.

3: THE VIKINGS AND BRIAN BORU

1 Ryan, *Irish monasticism*, p. vii, 316. There is an echo in the word 'manaig' of the eastern term 'sangha', which buddhists use to describe the whole community of practitioners. It is also spelt 'samgha' (*Encyclopaedia of Religion* at 'Samgha').

2 For later fishing on the Liffey see Went, 'Fisheries of the River Liffey', *passim* and Smyth, *Scandinavian York and Dublin*, pp. 207-8, 220 n. 83.

3 de Courcy, 'Looking at the Liffey in 795', pp. 16-18; Falkiner, 'Hospital', pp. 281-2. Falkiner cites Hogan to suggest that the name Kylmehanok or 'Kilmehanoc' derived from 'Cell-mo-samocc' (my sorrel). Is this more likely than that it comes from the name of a saint, as does 'Kilmacanogue' in Wicklow?

4 'Lec.109', cited at Hogan, *Onomasticon* at 'Cell Maignenn'. He also gives two references to one 'Mogobbog' at Kilmainham. Might this 'Cluain Rathach' be Clonraw, Co. Cavan, or Cloonragh, Co. Offaly? A big silver penannular brooch, dating from about AD 800 and regarded as one of the treasures of Ireland, has been discovered in Kilmainham (Nat. Mus. no. 45; DePaor, *Early Christian Ireland*, pp. 120-1). For a recent overview of the 'Golden Age' see Richter, *Medieval Ireland*, pp. 68-87.

27 The 'Kilmainham brooch'.

5 For more on Lerghus see Appendix C.
6 Taghmon is near where Wexford was subsequently founded by the Vikings. Today the site is as reduced as Maignenn's at Kilmainham (*Shell guide to Ireland*, p. 433). Meyer, *Triads*, p. xi (for dating of composition), pp. 4-5, no. 32, referring to 'tri tairleme Erenn'; ibid., pp. 6-7, no. 48 gives 'the three fords' of Ireland as Áth-Cliath, Athlone and Áth Caille [Woodford].
7 Bok, *Norse antiquities, passim*; Smyth, *Scandinavian York and Dublin*, pp. 207-8, 220 n. 83, 238-9, 256 n.; Clarke, *Medieval Dublin: the living city*, pp. 70-1; Healy, 'Con Colbert Road', p. 20; 'Viking Age Ireland', National Museum, exhibition of 1995; O'Brien, 'A tale of two cemeteries', pp. 13-17.
8 Richter, *Medieval Ireland*, p. 107, p. 115.
9 Haliday, *Scandinavian kingdom of Dublin*, pp. 1-5; Smyth, *Scandinavian York and Dublin*, pp. 238-9, 256 n.; *Cog. Gaedhel*, pp. 150-1 where it says 'he came to Cill-Maighnenn to the Green of Áth Cliath'.
10 For the murky history of Dublin before the tenth century see Ryan, 'Pre-Norman Dublin', pp. 64-8 and Clarke, 'Gaelic, Viking and Hiberno-Norse Dublin', pp. 8-19. The city existed before 988, although its 'millennium' was celebrated in 1988. Ryan believes that the Slige Cualann from Tara crossed the Liffey not at Áth Claith but at Leixlip, whence to Kilmainham. The 'eiscir riada', or ancient roadway of the charioteers, divided Ireland into two parts and is said to have extended from High Street in Dublin to Clarinbridge in Galway (Hogan, *Onomasticon*, p. 395). Eskers are glacial deposits and their elevation attracted early travellers. Although the gravel ridge of Kilmainham is not considered by the Geological Survey of Ireland to be an 'esker', its position ensured that it was the highway for many of those making their way to and from Áth Cliath. The Geological Survey has no record of any esker between Lucan and Dublin.
11 *Cog. Gaedhel*, pp. 150-1; Best, 'The Leabhar Oiris', p. 83, p. 90. The descendents of Niall Glúndubh took the family-name 'O'Neill'.
12 *Cog. Gaedhel*, p. 155. This text generally has been described as 'a singular wotk of medieval propaganda' and its author presumably viewed Brian's action as justifiable in the circumstances (Clarke, 'The Vikings in Ireland', p. 7).
13 *Dublin Evening Post*, 24 June 1802 noted that 'the cause of having bonfires on St John's Eve in this country is not well known – bonfires on hills was the signal on 23 June to begin at the same time the massacre of the Danes' (see also Danaher, *The year in Ireland*, pp. 152-3).
14 Ibid., p. 211; Best, 'Leabhar Oiris', p. 92.
15 Ibid; *Annals of Loch Cé* at AD 1014; Stuart, *Historical memoirs of the city of Armagh*, p. 123; Chatterton Newman, *Brian Boru*, p. 179.
16 Examples of the folk legend are *Dublin Penny Journal*, i (1832-3), pp. 68-9 and D'Alton, *County of Dublin*, pp. 605-6. The author of the former ('P' = George Petrie?) cites 'the Munster book of battles, by MacLiag' as authority for a statement that Murchadh was buried at 'the west end of the chapel, with a long stone standing on one end of his tomb, on which his name was written'. *Cog. Gaedhel*, which has sometimes been attributed to MacLiag, does not justify this and the *Penny Journal* itself confuses Armagh and Kilmainham. As early as the 1820s the legend concerning Brian and Murchadh had been described as 'quite erroneous' but it still persists, most recently accruing a 'quotation' from Murchadh

(Wright, *Historical guide to Dublin*, p. 189; Mac Thomáis, *Me jewel and darlin' Dublin*, p. 194).

17 Crawford, 'A descriptive list of early Irish crosses', p. 220; Henry, 'Early Christian slabs and pillar stones', 247-79; Sheehy, *Discovering Dingle*, p. 38 (Reask), p. 40 (Templenacloonagh), p. 45 (Kilvicadownaig); Sheehy, *Motorists guide to Dingle*, p. 24 (Currauley), p. 29 (Kilshannig). The particular interlace on the west side of the Kilmainham shaft appears to be unique. If there was once any decoration in the recesses of the north and south sides, respectively about 29 and 31 centimetres wide, it is no longer visible. Compare the shaft of Kilmainham with the crude ancient granite cross of Nethercross in Finglas (O'Broin, *Finglas*, pp. 9-11). For 'Scandinavian crosses' see Kermode, *Manx crosses*, pp. 142f.

18 Harbison, *High crosses of Ireland*, i, 130 and figs 435-6. From a sketch included in the *Dublin Penny Journal* article (n. 16 above) it appears that the shaft today stands as it did more than a century and a half ago; D'Alton, *County Dublin*, p. 605; Burton, *Royal Hospital*, p. 199 suggests that the cross is a 'sculpture of the eleventh century, not later'. Might it have been a market cross (Ó Maitiú, *Donnybrook*, p. 9)? The base is very irregular, being at the widest points 210 x 173 centimetres. The maximum height of the base above ground is today 25 centimetres.

19 Bourke, 'Early Irish hand-bells', p. 59; Anon., 'Bell of Kilmainham', pp. 39-43, including photograph of a bell found *c.*1844 during work on the railway, its exact location not being recorded. Said to be 'not older than twelfth century', it was in St Anne's Clontarf in 1900 but appears to be the bell now at National Museum, no. 1917-2. In a press cutting (n.d., n.l.) one 'William MacArthur' says that a bell found at Kilmainham was sold by the man who found it to 'Mr Murphy of Thomas St., the well-known bell founder, who preserved it for several years, afterwards presenting it to the late Sir Benjamin Lee Guinness'. It is then said to be at 'Ardilaun' (NLI Walshe MSS).

4: NORMAN KNIGHTS

1 D'Alton, *County Dublin*, p. 600.

2 Minahane, 'The knights of Kilmainham', pp. 15-21; Ware, *Antiquities of Ireland*, pp. 144-5; ibid. (accurate English translation, Dublin, 1705), p. 78. Ware was quite possibly guided by Alen (see n. 16 below). See also *Cal. anc. rec. Dublin*, i, 161 (AD 1261); Gilbert, *Hist. and municipal docs*, pp. lxxxiii-iv, 495-501.

3 *Rep. Nov.*, iii, no. 2 (1963-4), p. 254 n.; Stuart, 'Kilmainham, p. 26. Those who agree with Ware include Mills, 'The Norman settlement in Leinster', who rejects (pp. 168-9) as 'without authority' the suggestion that the Templars ever had the site; Falkiner, 'Hospital', *passim*; McNeill, Hospitallers', pp. 15-30; Gwynn and Hadcock, *Medieval religious houses*, p. 334f. The latter also suggest that the Templars did not even arrive in Ireland until 1180, when Strongbow was dead. See also Wood, 'Templars in Ireland', *passim*.

For the earlier error, sometimes still repeated in secondary works, see Alemand, *Histoire Monastique*, pp. 123-5; Alemand, *Mon. Hib.*, pp. 127-8; Colley, *Royal Hospital*, p. 12, p. 21; Archdall, *Mon. Hib.*, pp. xx-xxi, p. 222; Warburton, Whitelaw and Walsh, *Dublin*, p. 660; Lewis, *Topog. dict. Ire.*, i, 169; D'Alton, *County Dublin*, pp. 81, 534, 602-11. These authors tend to be confused and contradictory on the knights. Another glaring error by Alemand, was removed from his English translation (Kenny, 'Four Courts', p. 115).

4 *Cal. doc. Ire., 1171-1251*, p. 149, p. 171; *Cal. justic. rolls Ire., 1305-7*, p. 259; Gilbert, *Historical and municipal documents* , pp. 75-6, p. 79; McNeill, 'Hospitallers', p. 17; Ball, *County of Dublin*, iv, 179.

5 *Cal. doc. Ire., 1171-1251*, p. 22 (7 Nov. 1200); *Cal. anc. rec. Dublin*, i, 157 (1327), 193 (1603); ibid., xi, pp. 489f; Ware, *Antiquities* (ed. Harris, 1764), pp. 183-4; Fagan, *The second city*, p. 44.

6 *Cal. justic. rolls Ire., 1305-7*, pp. 481-3; *Cal. justic. rolls Ire., 1308-14*, p. 219.

7 *N.H.I.*, ii, 362; McNeill, 'Hospitallers', pp. 17-18; Kilmainham was the order's main house. Among other preceptories established were those at Kil[mainham]- beg and Kilmainham Wood in Co. Meath (Cogan, *Diocese of Meath*, i, 217-19; Falkiner, 'Hospital', pp. 311-12).

8 *Registrum de Kilmainham 1326-39*, p. vi, pp. vi-viii. For articles on the knights see Falkiner, McNeill and Minahane. There are also O'Dea and Lennox Barrow.

9 McNeill, 'Hospitallers', pp. 18-19.

10 Transcription of the *Registrum de Kilmainham* (R.I.A. MS), p. 25, p. 31, p. 35; *Registrum de Kilmainham 1326-39*, p. 23, p. 30 for a description of Rawlinson B.501 (Bodleain MS).

11 'Transcription', p. 109; *Reg. St John Dublin, passim*; McNeill, 'Hospital of St John without the Newgate'; Hennessy, 'Priory and hospital of Newgate', pp. 41-54. About 1420 money was raised by the king 'to build towers at the bridge of Kilmainham' (*Anal. Hib.*, ii (1931), p. 126). For more on the bridge see chapter 5, n. 3 below.

12 Transcription of *Registrum*, pp. 132-3; RHK minutes (National Archives MS) 1/1/1, p. 149 (6 March 1699); McNeill, 'Hospitallers, p. 20'; St John Joyce, *Neighbourhood of Dublin*, p. 347 says that the townland in which the leperhouse stood was known into the twentieth century as St Laurence and a fair used to be held there on St Laurence's Day.

13 D'Alton, *County Dublin*, pp. 617-18; Falkiner, 'Hospital', pp. 300-5; Bradshaw, *Dissolution of the religious orders*, pp. 28-9, 78-80, 122-3; Ellis, *Reform and revival*, pp. 46, 101, 132; Fitzsimons, 'Prior John Rawson', pp. 20-3. In 1495 a parliament at Drogheda passed an act to ensure that the prior of Kilmainham must be 'of the English blood' (*Anal. Hib.*, x (1941), p. 92).

14 *Extents Ir. mon. possessions*, p. 82.

15 Ibid., p. 81, p. 84; *Registrum de Kilmainham*, p. vi; Ronan, *The Reformation in Dublin*, p. 210; *Fiants Eliz., passim* refer to 'church-lands', 'the lands of the little/petty canons' and 'the procession mear' at Kilmainham.

16 Higgins, *Early Christian monuments of Galway*, i, 116 and fig. 41. 'Transcription of the *Registrum*', p. 89, p. 163; *Registrum de Kilmainham*, pp. 165-6; [Alen] *Reportorium Viride*, p. 184, p. 190; McNeill, 'Bodleian Library' at 'Rawl. B.479'. The image of the arm and anchor is recorded in a manuscript at Oxford which describes as follows 'fo.115' of an unidentified manuscript then 'in the public library, Cambridge':

> On this page there is a rude drawing of an anchor with a ring-head, held by a hand and sleeved-wrist issuing from a cloud with the letters ATHEMA, beneath the anchor, and this inscription beside it: 'In plurimis Prioratus fenestris depictu fuit brachium ex nube manutenens anchora':

and then in English: 'This arme out of a cloud houlding an anchor was paynted in many of the glass windows of Kilmaynham Priory before the demolishing thereof which was in the year 1612. By the word 'Athema' as I conceive was meant anathema'.

17 Walker, 'Memoir', p. 116; *R.S.A.I. Jn.*, v (1858-9), p. 444.

5: FROM PRINCELY CASTLE TO ROYAL HOSPITAL

1 Falkiner, 'Hospital', p. 305. Ellis, *Tudor Ireland*, p. 200, p. 210; *R.S.A.I.Jn.*, lii (1922), p. 14; *Anal. Hib.*, ii (1931), p. 140. Kilmainham was restored 8 March 1558, dissolved again 3 June 1559.
2 Letter, May 1559 (British Library MS); *Stat. Ire.*, 2 Eliz., c.7 (1560).
3 *Fiants Eliz.*, *passim* sub Kilmainham; *Cal. S.P. Irl.*, 1574-85, p. 52; Vigors, 'Merry Gallons', p. 96, p. 194; Falkiner, 'Phoenix Park', p. 468 for the report on decay from 'Ir. state papers 1572. Rec. office'. This is not in *Cal. S.P. Ire., 1509-73;* McNeill, 'Hospitallers', p. 19.
     Extents Ir. mon. possessions, p. 82; *Anal. Hib.*, x (1941), pp. 235-6; Crawford, *Anglicizing the government*, pp. 34, 57, 276; *H. M. C. Rep. De L'Isle & Dudley mss*, ii (1934), p. 31 gives 'warrant for payment of £20 to John Holman, as an imprest for the building of the bridge at Kilmainham, 18 Feb. 1576. Sidney's bridge was in use as late as 1791, when it was partly swept away by a flood. For Kilmainham bridge see D'Alton, *County Dublin*, p. 637; *R.S.A.I.Jn.*, lvi (1926), pp. 93-4; 'The Liffey bridges' (Ir. Arch. Arch.), pp. 63-7; O'Keeffe and Sinnington, *Irish stone bridges*, pp. 268-70.
4 *Anal. Hib.*, iv (1932), p. 309. This also refers to coals being carried from the meadow up to the castle. In May 1596 a commission was appointed to administer interrogatories concerning 'the common green of Kilmainham'. The answers of deponents survive (P.R.O.N.I. MS).
5 *Cal. S.P. Irl., 1603-6*, p. 195.
6 Letter of J. Strowde to the lord treasurer of England, concerning the dilapidation of Kilmainham (British Library, MS);*Cal. S.P. Irl., 1603-6*, p. 381, p. 524.
7 See chapter 4, n. 14 above; *Anal. Hib.*, xv (1944), p. 337.
8 'Oireachtas library: list of outlaws 1641-47' in *Anal. Hib.*, xxiii (1966), pp. 310-67.
9 *Civil Survey*, vii, 287, 292; There is no sign on Girdler's map of the 'great eastern tower beyond the walls of the castle of Kilmainham' which had been mentioned in the *Registrum* three hundred years earlier ('Transcription', p. 109).
10 Ch.4, n.15; Rocque, *Plan of Dublin and the environs*; RHK minutes, 1/1/5, f.175 and 1/1/7 (Trail's report of June 1795, considered further below) (National Archives MSS); Notes on Kilmainham plans (Ir. Arch. Arch., Murray collection).
11 Murphy, *Bully's Acre*, p. 17, p. 39 gives a headstone of the Hackets who died in 1652; Aalen and Whelan, *Dublin city and county,* p. 174; Ball, *County of Dublin*, iv, 158; *Census Ire., c.1659*, p. 379 which also gives population of Islandbridge (26), Inchicore (8), Dolphin's Barn (31).
12 Falkiner, 'Phoenix Park', pp. 464, 475-6; A survey of part of Newtowne and

Kilmainham left out of the Phoenix Park by making the wall straight, measured by Thomas Taylor, 1671 (Nat. Lib. Ire. MS).

13 RHK minutes, 1/1/7, p. 111; Ball, *County of Dublin*, iv, 157, 161, 184-90; Igoe and O'Dwyer, 'Early views of Kilmainham', pp. 78-87. It used to be thought that Sir Christopher Wren designed the Royal Hospital (*Ir. Builder*, 31 May 1924).

14 Colley, *Foundation of the Royal Hospital*, p. 17, p. 20; Harris, *Dublin*, p. 426; Lennox Barrow, 'Knights Hospitaller', p. 109.

15 Ir. Arch. Arch., photographs no. 5/18X3 & 5/18Y9; Wilkinson, *Geology and ancient architecture in Ireland*, p. 105, p. 117, p. 245.

16 Chart, *Story of Dublin*, p. 200; Craig, *Architecture of Ireland*, p. 154.

17 *Cal. S.P. dom.,1698*, pp. 243-4. MacLysaght, *Ir. life*, pp. 389-90. In December 1670 an indictment at Kilmainham had been threatened in a more mundane matter relating to weights and measures (*Cal. anc. rec. Dublin*).

18 Ball, *County of Dublin*, iv, 159 citing Carte papers, cliv, 71; Igoe and O'Dwyer, 'Early views of the Royal Hospital, Kilmainham', pp. 78-88, who explain why the detail of Islandbridge is shown differently in each.

19 Igoe and O'Dwyer, 'Early views of Kilmainham', pp. 80-1.

6: THE HOLY WELL OF ST JOHN

1 Neary, 'Pilgrimages to sacred wells', pp. 272-9; Brenneman, *Crossing the circle at the holy wells of Ireland, passim*. This is an interesting phenomenological study.

2 *S.P. Hen. VIII*, iii, 1 (Browne to Alen); Bradshaw, 'George Browne', pp. 301-26; Lennon, *Sixteenth century*, pp. 138-9. D'Alton, *County Dublin*, gives 'patrons' [patterns?] for 'pardons' but see text further.

3 See chapter 4, n. 13 above. Donnelly, *Dublin parishes*, ii, pp. 204-5. The priory had also won exemption from certain taxes (*Anal. Hib.*, ii (1931), p. 127).

4 *S.P. Hen. VIII*, iii, 5, 35; Cogan, *Diocese of Meath*, i, pp. 88-100; Neary, 'Pilgrimages to sacred wells', p. 277 quotes Rothe on a devotion on the eve of St Michael. At St John's Well, Kilkenny, there was formerly a church only big enough for the priest and his servers. It stood in a graveyard thirty yards from the well. There was also a pulpit in the graveyard. A dove was said to descend at midnight on St John's Eve and invalids were thereupon cured. Having been suppressed by the bishop in 1761 it was revived but due to disorder was supressed again in 1834-5 (Wells of Leinster (U.C.D. MSS. These are quoted by kind permission of the head of the Department of Irish Folklore, U.C.D.)).

5 In 1729 St Patrick's Well ran dry, reportedly due to inappropriate behaviour by some of the devotees (Warburton, Whitelaw & Walsh, *Dublin*, i, pp. 244-5; *Dublin Gazette*, 25-9 March 1729, reprinted at *Report. Nov.* iii (1962), p. 218; Ball, 'St Patrick's Well', p. 187). For other wells of St Patrick in Dublin see *R.I.A. Proc.*, vii (1857-61), p. 264.

6 *Dublin Daily Post* (21 July 1710).

7 Cogan, *Diocese of Meath*, ii, 351; *Commons' Jn. Ire.* (ed. Dublin, 1796), pp. 669-70. On the same day the Commons unanimously passed a resolution for 'the strict and due execution of the several laws in force against sturdy beggars and vagrants, and for confining the poor thereof to their respective parishes'. On 15

June 1783 a prohibition was read from the altars of Dublin relating to St John's Well in County of Meath (*Report Nov.*, ii, pp. 169-70).

The well at Kilmainham is barely two miles from Dublin Castle, whereas that at Warrenstown, near Dunshaughlin, is about twenty miles away. 'Fourteen' old 'Irish miles' (2240 yds) were about eighteen standard miles (1760 yds). The 'beautiful spring' at Warrenstown was mentioned by John Lynch in 1662 and in the 1860s Cogan (above) wrote of 'St John's Well, at which stations used to be had, which were frequented by great numbers of people. This well is only a few perches distant from the place where mass was celebrated during penal times'. In 1944 the well was 'rebuilt' in the style of the day but some of the old seats and slabs and two small stone heads remain. It is near Warrenstown College and is still visited today on both the eve and day of St John and on the following Sunday. In 1995 about sixty people attended for devotions (*Cambr. ev.*, i, 132-2).

Report Nov., ii, p. 68, p. 71, p. 74, p. 123 indicates the existence of six wells of St John in County Dublin, of which two were in the city.

8 Burke, 'Secret church', p. 81. In 1719 a Fr Conner was among four 'Popish priests taken out of a mass-house of this city' of Dublin. He was committed to Kilmainham gaol (*Arch. Hib.*, xvi (1951), p. 33).

9 Murphy, *Bully's Acre*, p. 15, p. 43; RHK minutes 1/1/1, p. 251 (1704); Burton, *Royal Hospital*, pp. 197-8. In 1698 Dunton wrote of the Royal Hospital after the battle of Aughrim that 'there were 1200 sick and wounded men in it, but then the hall and galleries had beds laid in them'. The Royal Hospital would normally house between three and four hundred (MacLysaght, *Ir. life*, p. 389).

10 RHK minutes, 1/1/1, p. 125. It was noted that the 'nasty men' were to have straw rather than matresses, presumably being incontinent.

11 RHK minutes, 1/1/4, p. 191.

12 Ibid., 1/1/5, p. 173 (5 Nov. 1763); *Ir. Builder*, 1 Dec. 1896; Igoe and O'Dwyer, 'Early views', p. 81. Henry Massue, earl of Gal[l]way (*d.*1720) was one of the lords justices in 1697.

13 Nowlan, 'Kilmainham Jail', p. 107; RHK minutes, 1/1/7, pp. 112-14 (22 June 1795). Trail could not find a survey map of the lands which Wm Robinson drew in 1681 (see RHK minutes 1/1/1, f.221 (4 March 1702-3)).

14 *Dublin Chronicle*, 23 June 1787 (also at *Archiv. Hib.*, xviii (1955), p. 256); Burke, 'A secret church?', pp. 82-92; *Report. Nov.*, ii (1958), p. 171; MacGiolla Phádraig, 'Dr John Carpenter', p. 11.

15 [L'Estrange], 'John's Well in the olden time: a sketch from real life'. See also chapter 8, n. 25.

16 Ó Danachair, 'The holy wells of Co. Dublin', p. 69. A suggestion by Sweeney that it was also called 'Groynyor's Well' is mistaken (Sweeney, *Rivers of Dublin*, p. 109; Mr Sweeney in conversation with this author, August 1995).

17 *Historical and municipal documents*, p. xli, p. 62; *Dublin Evening Post*, 1 July 1834; Ó Maitiú, *Donnybrook*, pp. 8-10; chapter 4, n. 11 above. If the order of 1204 was intended to refer to Drogheda then it seems odd that a further order of 1221 explicitly refers to the establishment of an 8-day fair at Drogheda to coincide with the feast of the apostles, Saints Peter and Paul, on 29 June (*Cal. doc. Ire.*, 1171-1251, at 29 July 1221).

7: ST JOHN'S EVE

1 MacNeill has associated 'Garland Sunday' with the Celtic festival of Lughnasa
   (1 August). See a curious comment to the Folklore Commission in 1943 from
   Longford: 'I also remember the old people saying there were two St John's
   Eve's, one right and one wrong. The second was at the same date in July,
   namely the 24th'. Was this a folk memory of the church re-directing midsum-
   mer celebrations away from the 'wrong' end of July (Lughnasa) to the 'right'
   end of June (St John's)? Mí-meán (mee-mahan) is one of the Irish names for
   June and, in Offaly, the feast was also known as 'Mi-mheadhon'. Elsewhere
   'John' became 'Owen' . Cordner notes other examples of celebrations at holy
   wells which did not always coincide with the feast of the associated saint (Cordner,
   'The cult of the holy well', p. 36; Danaher, 'June', p. 146; St John's Eve (U.C.D.
   MSS, quoted by kind permission of the head of the Department of Irish Folklore, U.C.D.), p. 72, p. 103, p. 112).
2 Cogan, *Diocese of Meath*, ii, 510.
3 MacNeill, *Lughnasa*, p. 603 for Struel Wells, Co. Down, where by 1836 the
   face was 'nearly worn away'.
4 Burton, *Royal Hospital*, p. 199; MacNeill, *Lughnasa*, p. 603; Murphy, *Bully's
   Acre*, p. 7; Weir, *Early Ireland: a field guide*, p. 140. Harbison, *High crosses*, i, 130
   and figs 435-6.
5 *Dublin Newsletter*, 13-16 March 1742; Archdall, *Mon. Hib.*, p. 205 who says that
   on St John's day 'a great bonfire was made before the hospital [of St John at
   Newgate] and many others throughout the city'; Fagan, *The second city*, p. 49.
6 Joyce, *Neighbourhood of Dublin*, pp. 203-4.
7 Crofton Croker, *Researches in the south of Ireland*, pp. 277-83, also cited at Dixon
   Hardy, *Holy wells of Ireland*, pp. 49-53. MacNeill, *Lughnasa*, p. 603 says Hardy
   'wrote with strong antipathy to the popular devotions of the Catholic peasantry
   but for that very reason described them as minutely as he could'. He did not
   mention the Kilmainham well.
8 St John's Eve (U.C.D. MSS).
9 O'Rahilly, *Early Irish history*, p. 172.
10 For more on midsummer customs see Danaher, 'June', pp. 145-8; Danaher,
   The year in Ireland, pp. 134-53.
11 *Dublin Evening Post*, 24 June 1802.

8: NEW KILMAINHAM

1 *Faulkner's Journal*, 23-27 July 1751; *Ir. Builder*, 1 Feb. 1895; Ball, *County of Dublin*, iv,160-2. For the endemic riots between these factions see Fagan, *The second
   city*, pp. 46-9.
2 Ardagh, 'A Dublin statue to Shakespeare', p. 24; Keenahan, 'The Shakespeare
   House, Old Kilmainham', pp. 33-5. For the active use, 'they'd justice him at
   Kilmainham', see Staples, *Sir Jonah Barrington*, p. 106. The site of the gaol at old
   Kilmainham appeared on ordnance survey maps into the twentieth century.
3 Sleator's *Public Gazetteer*, vii, 178.
4 Press-clipping in Cuttings by R.D.Walshe (NLI MSS), apparently from *The
   Town and Country Weekly Magazine*.

5 Ibid., for further cuttings from the same source; *Evening Telegraph*, 16 and 23 Sept. 1911. These Annesleys were involved in a famous peerage case (Ball, *County of Dublin*, iv, 160).

6 Ibid. This was notwithstanding the fact that one week earlier 'a man called Wilde was hanged at Kilmainham common for stopping and cutting Mr Gunning, with intent to rob him'.

7 Ibid. Unidentified cutting.

8 Faulkner's *Dublin Journal*, 13 Aug. 1796; *Ir. Builder*, 1 Feb. 1895; Nowlan, 'Kilmainham Jail', pp. 105-15, states that the symbolism of the serpents is 'unknown'; Kelly, *Kilmainham Gaol, passim*; Kilmainham Jail Restoration Society, *Kilmainham: the Bastille of Ireland*, p. 3; Cooke, *Kilmainham Gaol*, p. 7, p. 17.

9 Conaghan et al., *The Grand Canal*, p. 17. For Sarah Bridge, Kilmainham, showing to the west the older Island Bridge, built in 1578 on the site of an even older bridge see *Sentimental and Masonic Magazine*, i (reproduced at Fagan, *The second city*, p. 26). In 1763 an act of parliament set up commissioners for making the Circular Road (*Stat. Ire.*, 3 Geo. II, c.36).

10 Sleator's *Public Gazetteer*, 5-9 Dec. 1769; *Freeman's Journal*, April 1799; *Archiv. Hib.*, xvii (1953), p. 122. See also n. 25 below.

11 RHK minutes, 1/1/7, p. 109 (1795). Murphy, *Bully's Acre*, pp. 18-32 indicates that in the 1780s and 1790s some people continued to be buried in a proper style at Bully's Acre, as may be seen from surviving headstones, including those of Robert Brown, mohair throster and twister, and Phillip Rielly, starch manufacturer. The area used by catholics was perhaps a little to the west and north of that in which the headstones stand.

12 For Malton see Igoe and O'Dwyer, 'Early views of the Royal Hospital', pp. 84-5.

13 The environs of Dublin surveyed by Thomas Campbell, under the direction of Major Taylor, AD 1811 (King's Inns library). For the well see also chapter 9, n. 11 below; A survey of the Royal Hospital Lands at Kilmainham by Wm Murray, 10 Oct. 1839 (National Archives, RHK MS 9/1/3).

14 'Fingal', 'The Liffey from its source', p. 77 (1 March 1883).

15 Cutting (n.d., n.l.) in Walshe (NLI MS). Perhaps the nickname 'Bully' is somehow connected with Bully's Acre.

16 *Dublin Evening Post*, 27 Nov. 1802.

17 *Freeman's Jn.*, 5-6 May 1812; Fagan, *Second city*, pp. 39-40.

18 Lewis, *Topog. dict. Ire.*, at Kilmainham; Costelloe, *Churches of Dublin*, p. 186. Non-conformists in the area had both the Independent Meeting House and the Salem Chapel.

19 Daly, *Dublin*, p. 171.

20 *Ir. Builder*, 1 June 1867; *Evening Telegraph*, 5 March 1921; Jago, 'Kilmainham court-house' (U.C.D. MS thesis).

21 G.S. & W. Railway, minute book 3, 12 March 1845 to 4 August 1846 (C.I.E. MS), p. 201); *Irish Builder*, 1 Dec. 1896; Igoe and O'Dwyer, 'Early views of the Royal Hospital', p. 85, p. 87 for Sadler in colour.

22 RHK Minutes, 1/1/17, pp. 183, 194; *Irish Builder*, 15 Nov. 1879; *Ir. Builder*, 1 Dec. 1896; Craig, *Dublin*, 285. See p. 114 below.

23 Cromwell, *Excursions through Ireland*, pp. 178-9.

24 Mc Gregor, *Picture of Dublin*, p. 313.

25 Cromwell, *Excursions*, pp. 178-9; Meyler, *St Catherine's Bells*, i, 33, 73-4;

Cameron, 'Recollections of a long life', p. 7; Childers, and Stewart, *Royal Hospital Kilmainham*, pp. 28-9; Anon., 'Bully's Acre and body-snatchers', pp. 7-8.

26 D'Alton, *County Dublin*, p. 602 suggested that, before it closed, the cemetery was perhaps 'the most extensive in the British Empire, comprising 3 acres and a half old Irish measure'; Barry, *Glasnevin Cemetery*, p. 2; Murphy, *Bully's Acre*, p. 12; Egan, 'Memorials of the dead' (Nat. Archives), pp. 1-3; Corcoran, 'Goldenbridge cemetery', pp. 11-13.

27 [L'Estrange], 'John's Well in the olden times', *passim.*

28 'Fingal', 'The Liffey from its source', p. 77.

29 [Seaton], *Kilmainham Pensioner's Lament.* There is a copy of this rare pamphlet in the National Library. For reproductions of some of its engravings see Stuart, 'Kilmainham', p. 25, p. 36; *Dublin Penny Journal*, p. 218 (9 Jan. 1836); *Second report of committee on Chelsea and Kilmainham, 1871.*

30 *Report of the committee on intoxication*, 1834, p. 442.

31 Burke, *Popular culture in early modern Europe*, ch. 8; Ó Maitiú, *Donnybrook*, pp. 34-52.

32 'Letter from E. Curry, 1837' in 'Ordnance survey letters: Dublin', (Nat. Lib. Irl. typescript), pp. 49-50.

33 Burton, *Royal Hospital*, pp. 10-11.

9: VICTORIAN PROGRESS

1 Lewis, *Topog. dict. Ire.*, at Islandbridge.

2 D'Alton, *County Dublin*, pp. 632-3.

3 'Fingal', 'The Liffey from its source', p. 77. 'Rowling' is an obsolete form of 'rolling', which itself was sometimes used for 'bowling' (*O.E.D.*)

4 Corish, 'The Catholic community in the nineteenth century', p. 26. Examples of the suppression of wells include, in 1834-5, St John's Well, Kilkenny, 'due to disorder'. In 1848 Kelly wrote that 'within the past few years' the 'patron' at St John's Well, Meath, was prohibited, 'because too many people came for amusement'. In 1874 the 'patron' of St Maelruain at Tallaght was ended (*Camb. ev.*, i, 133n; Joyce, *Neighbourhood of Dublin*, pp. 203-4).

5 Burton, *Royal Hospital*, p. 199. Hall, *Ireland*, i, 279-82 includes about this time a fine sketch of the 'far-famed' well of St Dolough at Malahide, Co. Dublin, but has nothing on St John's Well. Robert Cunningham was master of the RHK, 1793-6. For 'the waters of Shiloah [Siloam] that flow gently' see *Isa.* 8:6, *John* 9: 7, 11 and Black's *Bible Dictionary* (8th ed., 1973), pp. 683-4.

6 RHK minutes, 1/1/17 *passim*, with quotation at p. 149; ibid., p. 287 notes that in October 1844 the company applied for the first time to construct a terminus on hospital lands and did so again in January 1845; 'An Act for making and maintaining a railway from the city of Dublin to the town of Cashel, with a branch to the town of Carlow' (7 & 8 Vict., c.10). The line would ultimately by-pass Cashel. For the company's acquisition of 'the town and lands of Inchicore' see 'Caldwell et. al. to Great Southern and Western Railway Company, 1848' (Registry of Deeds, no. 1/176/17).

7 *Irish Railway Gazette*, 10 Feb. & 22 Sept. 1845, 23 March, 20 & 27 July, 10 Aug. 1846; *Dublin Evening Post*, 4 Aug. 1846; Sheehy, *Kingsbridge Station*, p. 4

8 D'Alton, *A memoir of the Great Southern & Western Railway*, p. 12; *Ir. Builder*, 15 Nov. 1879; *Ir. Builder*, 1 Dec. 1896. See p. 114 below.

9 RHK minutes, 1/1/17, pp. 183, 194, 425, 446-7, 532; ibid., pp. 446-7 also show that a road where St John's Road West was later to be built was under consideration as early as 1846; Igoe and O'Dwyer, 'Early views', p. 87. Sadler clearly includes the old bridge over the Camac; Jacob, 'Kingsbridge Terminus', p. 115. In 1845 the Board of Public Works took over the responsibility for maintaining the Royal Hospital (Catalogue to the Murray Collection (Ir. Arch. Arch. MS), p. 133).

10 D'Alton, *Memoir*, p. 29; G. S. & W. Railway Co., minute book 3 (C.I.E. MS, p. 252).

11 'A guide to St John's House' (Order of Matla typescript). According to this the font was removed to the church of St James in 1844. It was not mentioned in the newspaper report of the foundation ceremony. O'Connell told those assembled that, amongst other things, 'to an Irish catholic bigotry was unknown' (*Freeman's Journal*, 5 April 1844). The surround of granite blocks, eight feet high, remains at St James and is said to have once sheltered there a statue of St John.

12 O.S. map, south Dublin. 'surveyed 1838, engraved 1846-7' (Valuation Office); The sketch, signed and dated by Wakeman, appears in an unidentified press-cutting (NLI Walshe MS) and was to be reproduced at Joyce, *Neighbourhood of Dublin*, pp. 341-3.

13 Thom's *Directory*, 1869, p. 1922. A brass plaque was erected to commemorate the royal visit. It is kept today in the rooms of the archivist at the Royal Hospital (For an unsatisfactory photograph of it see Ir. Arch. Arch. 5/18X39). Bloody Bridge was renamed Victoria and Albert Bridge. In 1903 Edward VII visited the Royal Hospital (*Ireland Illustrated*, August 1903).

14 *Ir. Builder*, 1 June 1867; Kennedy, *Sanitary arrangements*. Kennedy, with rooms at Merrion Square and his residence at Belgard Castle, Clondalkin, was a very distinguished authority on health and one of a trio of remarkable brothers from Derry (Thom's *Directory*, 1867; Kenny, 'Honest Tristram Kennedy').

15 *Evidence* and *Report of the boundaries commission* 1880-1.

16 Daly, *Dublin*, p. 159, p. 170. The author adds that the population of Kilmainham contained 'an unexpectedly high number of Protestants', but her own statistics show that at 65-7% the percentage of Catholics was not low when compared to that in the other suburbs (p. 149, p. 171).

17 *Report of the boundaries commission*, report, ev. 5773; Costello, *Churches of Dublin*, p. 156. There are listed 'Papers relating to Inchicore Catholic Club, 1898' (National Archives).

18 31 & 32 Vict., c.110; Daly, *Dublin*, p. 159, p. 282. The records of Kilmainham Township appear to have been lost. Dublin Corporation holds those for some other suburban townships.

19 Cutting (n.d., n.l.) in Walshe (NLI MS); *New concise British flora*, plates 2, 13, 50, 84. The plants mentioned are common.

20 'St Patrick's Home: a day in the life of Kilmainham Institution' in *Ev. Telegraph* (16 Sept. 1922).

21 Cutting (n.d., n.l.) in Walshe (NLI MS); Malcolm, *'Ireland sober, Ireland free'*, pp. 189-90. In 1846 and 1847 Spratt and others harangued fair-goers from a platform in Donnybrook (Ó Maitiú, *Donnybrook*, pp. 42-3).

22 Cutting (n.l., 25 June 1886) in Walshe (NLI MS).
23 *Ir. Builder*, 1 Dec. 1896.
24 Joyce, *Neighbourhood of Dublin*, pp. 341-3. The ordnance survey map which shows the well is that which in 1902 was 'transferred' by Harry Lisney from a version of 1889. Both it and that of 1907 are reference National Grid, XVIII, nos 54 & 64.

The gardens were included for the first time in Thom's *Directory* in 1898, under 'St John's Gardens, St John's Road, Islandbridge'. Joyce mistakenly calls them 'St John's Terrace', confusing the name of the terrace with another further south and across South Circular Road, which was 'St John's Terrace'.

On some old maps this portion of the Circular Road at St John's Gardens is given as 'St John's Road' – not to be confused with St John's Road West which runs from the railway station to the railway bridge across the S. C. Rd. – and even as O'Connell Road which, until 1900, was the name of a section of the S. C. Rd. near Richmond Hill.

25 'St John's Gardens, Kilmainham' (Nat. Lib. Ire., 16 G.14. (25)).

10: THE TWENTIETH-CENTURY.

1 *Report of the boundaries commission,* report and ev. 5709-6198; Daly, *Dublin,* pp. 226-39.
2 *Ireland Illustrated,* December 1900; *Irish Literary Gazette,* April 1851 (reporting a debate of 28 March); *Report of the committee on Chelsea and Kilmainham,* 1883 and *Report of War Office committee on Chelsea and Kilmainham,* 1894, *passim.*
3 *The Lady of the House,* 15 September 1893. In the National Library are manuscripts known as 'the Kilmainham papers'. These are the correspondence of the commander-in-chief of the British forces in Ireland, 1782-1890. Although the commander resided at Kilmainham these papers generally refer to a range of matters of no immediate local relevance.
4 *Evening Telegraph,* 1 Aug. 1908; De L. Smyth, *A site for the new university, passim.* The Lawrence photograph of the Dublin University boat-club (Royal no. 6217), reproduced above, shows Inchicore Road behind, with St Jude's Church visible. In 1906 one young Church of Ireland parishioner wrote of St Jude's that 'it makes a pretty picture', but demolition overtook it in 1988 (Costelloe, *Churches of Dublin,* p. 230).
5 Childers and Stewart, *Royal Hospital,* p. 54; Cooke, *Kilmainham Gaol,* pp. 30-41. For a stirring view of the gaol's place in our political history see Kilmainham Jail Restoration Society, *Ghosts of Kilmainham.* More restrained is the same society's *Kilmainham: the Bastille of Ireland.* The gaol is frequently used as a film-set.
6 Ibid., p. 76; *Irish Times,* 18 Dec. 1922. For photographs which show some of the armour and guns see the Lawrence collection (NLI Royal no. 4022), *Ireland Illustrated,* Dec. 1900, above p. 83) and *Irish Life,* 29 Sept. 1916. In a letter to the *Irish Times* (30 Dec. 1922), T.P. Stuart expressed his concern about the fate of a sword found in the late eighteenth century 'on a tiled floor' in the grounds of the Royal Hospital. He pointed out that it was absent from a list of weapons at the Royal Hospital which Childers had compiled in 1892 (Childers and Stewart, *Royal Hospital,* p. 76) and assumed that it had been taken to England. In 1786

Walker had identified this as a 'Templar' sword and invited readers to compare a sketch of it with that of a sword on a Templar's tomb. In fact the two appear quite dissimilar and that found at Kilmainham more closely resembles subsequent Viking finds in the area. There is in 1832 another reference, ostensibly to the same sword, but the sketch accompanying the second reference differs from that by Walker, the sword being shown as much shorter and having a different handle. In 1832 this sword was said to be hanging in the commander's rooms at the Royal Hospital but in 1941 a thorough enquiry by a member of the Gardai failed to locate it and the National Museum cannot say where it is (Walker, 'Memoir', p. 116; *Dublin Penny Journal* (1832-3), p. 69; O'Reily, 'Garda headquarters, Kilmainham').

7 *Freeman's Journal*, 11 July 1923.
8 *Manchester Guardian*, 31 March 1923.
9 Letter from J.G. Swift MacNeill in *Irish Times*, 20 July 1923; *Evening Telegraph*, 11 July 1923; *Freeman's Journal*, 24 January 1924.
10 Childers and Stewart, *Royal Hospital*, p. 55.
11 *Evening Telegraph*, 18 March 1911; *Freeman's Journal*, 3 November 1924. The site of the disused court-house in old Kilmainham, on the tramline near the Camac, was sold off only at the turn of the century and in Thom's *Directory* of 1900 it is noted that there were then six cottages inside the enclosure of the original gaol, of which the massive granite blocks of the front boundary were still in place. The location is marked on o.s. maps.
12 *Irish Times*, 18, 19 June 1924, 15 Jan. 1925; *Freeman's Journal*, 1 Dec. 1924; See also Hurley, 'St Michael's C.B.S., Keogh Square and Richmond Barracks', pp. 25-7. For the garrison church see McGuirk, 'St Michael's Church, Inchicore', pp. 7-8.
13 Ó Danachair, 'Holy well legends in Ireland', p. 39. For a recent account of preservation stories see Lynch, 'The holy wells of Wicklow', pp. 633-4.
14 O'Meara, *Giraldus Cambrensis*, p. 63.
15 Neary, 'Pilgrimages to sacred wells', p. 277.
16 Ibid., p. 274; *Camb. ev, i*, 129.
17 Costello, *Churches of Dublin*, p. 156.
18 Ó Danachair, 'Holy well legends', p. 35; *Camb. ev.*, i, 132-3; Brenneman, *Holy wells of Ireland*, p. 7. For more on holy wells see Gribben, *Holy wells and sacred water sources in Britain and Ireland: an annotated bibliography*.
19 Pastoral letter of the bishops of Ireland on the occasion of Famine Remembrance Sunday, 24 Sept. 1995, paragraph 17.
20 Ó Danachair, 'The holy wells of County Dublin', p. 80. One of the present residents of 685 S. C. Rd., which is the house at St John's Gardens beside the former site of the well, told this author that before the laneway by that house was tarred she inspected it and saw what she took to be an opening filled with concrete. It is now completely covered by a tarred surface. The residents recall no flat slab such as that which St John Joyce noted. They thought that the lane might be the property of the catholic archdiocese of Dublin but Mgr John Wilson, financial administrator of the archdiocese, has informed this author that it does not appear to be the case. He adds, 'There will often be a view from residents, because of a holy well or other similar item of interest, that the Church is the owner of the property itself, or of the adjoining roads or laneways' (Letter to author, 6 Sept. 1995).

21 Warburton, Whitelaw and Walsh, *History of the city of Dublin*, p. 667. The authors recall that water had been brought to the hospital in wooden pipes which passed through the cemetery and that there was a 'general prejudice' against that system!

It was Akong Rinpoche, abbot of Dolma Lhakang monastery in Tibet and of Samye Ling monastery in Dumfriesshire, Scotland, who recently divined the spring. An opening was made for it in June 1995 (O'Neill, *The Well, i, 6*). 'Kilmainham Well House', or 56 Inchicore Road (also '2, The Laurels'), is on the map of 1902 mentioned at chapter 9, n. 24 above.

EPILOGUE

1 Childers and Stewart, *Royal Hospital*, p. 22.
2 Bersu file (Nat. Museum MS); Eames and Fanning, *Irish medieval tiles*, p. 63 and illustrations L4-6, L20, L76-77. Fanning gives L2 as a design of a lion passant, gardant in frame, found uniquely in Kilmainham but it is in fact a griffon from a tile at Greatconnell, Co. Kildare. For a fine colour photograph of types L4-5 in situ in a floor at Swords see p. 41 of Eames and Fanning.
3 For the restoration of the Royal Hospital from 1980 see, *inter alia*, Costello, Murray & Beaumont, *Royal Hospital Kilmainham*; Olley, 'The narrative at Kilmainham'. In May 1991 the Royal Hospital became the Irish Museum of Modern Art.
4 Harbison, *High crosses*, i, 130.
5 Office of Public Works, file on Kilmainham, including a report of June 1981 which states: 'There are undoubtedly human remains under the tarred avenue leading from the Royal Hospital toward Kilmainham'. While digging a hole to bury some bones found during work on the avenue there were discovered several slabs in Bully's Acre. These were deemed to have been possibly simple grave-markers and of 'no archaeological interest'.

The author is grateful for information to Mr Paddy Healy, who in 1991 supervised roadworks for Dublin Corporation, when 'vast, vast quantities of bone' were disturbed and then reburied. Healy says that the earth at Bully's Acre has been greatly disturbed to a depth of six feet. Healy found no sign of the old well itself in the area then dug up.

APPENDIX A

1 *Martyrology of Tallaght, Martyrology of Oengus; Martyrology of Donegal; Martyrology of Gorman*; Carrigan, *Diocese of Ossory*, ii, 132 & iv, 240; O'Hanlon, *Lives,* xi (19 Oct.). O'Hanlon's work ended prematurely and so there is no principal entry for Maignenn.
2 *Acta S.S.*, p. 584 (11 March).
3 O'Hanlon, *Lives*, iv (1 April); Byrne, *Irish kings and high-kings* (London, 1973), pp. 72-4, 120-1.
4 *Martyrology of Donegal* (18 Dec.).
5 Ibid., (26 March); O'Hanlon, *Lives,* iii (26 March for Sincheall and Liffey), ix (12 Sept. for Ailbe); *Cog. Gaedhel*, p. lxx, p. 22 n. 5 says that 'Cluain Daimh'

[*sic*] signifies 'Plain or lawn of the Deer or Oxen'. The writer locates it, thus spelt, in Meath. Is it possible, however, that the name is an early version of 'Clondalkin', where the remains of an old church were recently found and about the origins of which there appears to be a doubt? (Rynne, 'Excavation of a Church-site at Clondalkin', pp. 29-37)?; Clarke, *Medieval Dublin: the making of a metropolis*, p. 63; Sharpe, 'Quatuor sanctissimi', pp. 376-99.

6 Letter to the author, dated Dublin, 3 July 1995. Also see Ó Riain, *Corpus Genealogiarum*, ss 54, 662.91, 705.22, 707.822, 722.90.

7 MacCana, *Celtic Mythology*, p. 34, p. 79; MacNeill, *Lughnasa*, p. 353; Ó hOgain, *Myth, Legend and Romance*, pp. 286-9.

APPENDIX B

1 British Library, Egerton MS 91, old 'f.108' but now f. 49; Bibliothèque Nationale, Fonds Celtique et Basque, MS 1, ff 30-2.

2 Todd, 'Report on Irish MSS', p. 226; Omont, *Catalogue* (also in in *Revue Celtique*, xi (Paris, 1890)), p. 10; Kenney, *Sources*, p. 466; O'Grady (ed.), *Silva Gad.*, i, 37ff and ii, 35ff.

3 Two sequences from the 'Account' of Maignenn were translated earlier than O'Grady (*Martyrology of Donegal*, pp. 338-41; O'Curry, *Manners and customs*, p. ccxl).

4 Sharpe, *Medieval Irish saint's lives*; Letter to the author, dated Oxford, 21 July 1995.

5 O'Grady, *Silva. Gad.*, ii, p. vii; Flower,*Catalogue*, ii, 446. The first volume of the *Catalogue* was edited by O'Grady; Kenney, *Sources*, p. 466.

6 *Martyrology of Oengus*, p. 45; Book of Hy Many (R.I.A. MS, fourteenth century).

7 Ó hOgain, *Encyclopaeia of the Irish folk tradition*, p. 28, pp. 235-6.

8 O'Hanlon, *Lives*, i (16 Jan.).

APPENDIX C

1 Kendrick, *Druids*, p. 16 n.

2 *Dict. Ir. Lang.* at 'iccaidh'; Davies, 'Healing in early Irish society', p. 49.

3 D'Alton, *County Dublin*, p. 604; Bennett, *Encyclopaedia of Dublin*, at Kilmainham, gives 'philosopher'.

4 Richter, *Medieval Ireland*, pp. 71-5.

5 Medieval tracts and recipes, with some collections on experimental science [etc] (British Library MS).

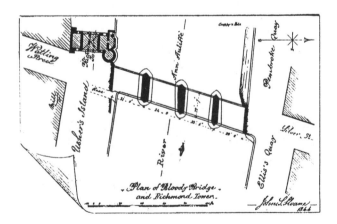

28 Richmond Gate and Guard Tower, before 1846. Moved in 1846 to its
present location near Kilaminham Gaol, the gate had earlier stood at
the western end of the south quays between Watling Street and Bloody
Bridge. It marked the start of the Military Road to the Royal Hospital.

Bibliography

MANUSCRIPTS AND TYPESCRIPTS

Bibliothèque National, Paris
Betha Maignenn (Fonds Celtique et Basque, MS 1, ff 30-32).

British Library
Account of the sayings and doings of Saint Magniu or Maignenn of Kilmainham,
    Co. Dublin (Egerton MS 91, old 'f.108', new f. 49).
Medieval tracts and recipes, with some collections on experimental science, chiefly
    in Latin, made perhaps by a resident in Ireland. References to St Columkill and
    to Kilmainham, Co. Dublin. Fourteenth century (Royal MS 12. B. xxv; Nat.
    Lib. of Ire. P.1452 for a good microfilm copy of this).
Letter, May 1559 (Lansdowne MS 159, f.108).
Letter of J. Strowde to the earl of Dorset, lord treasurer of England, concerning the
    dilapidation of Kilmainham, the ruinous residence of the lord deputy (Lansdowne
    MS 159, f.254).
Annals of Clonmacnoise translated into English AD 1627 by Conell Mageoghagan
    (Add. MS 4797, f.48).
Annals in Irish from the year 457 (Clarendon MSS, Add. MS 4784, ff 36-86).

Córas Iompair Éireann
Great Southern & Western Railway, minute book 3, 12 March 1845 to 4 August
    1846 (Heuston Station MS).

Irish Architectural Archive
Royal Hospital Kilmainham, surveys and notes (William Murray collection)
The Liffey bridges from Islandbridge to East Link: a historical and technological
    report compiled by the Liffey Bridges Survey Team (D.Dub.1.99).

National Archives
Royal Hospital Kilmainham, minutes, papers and maps.
Papers relating to the premises of Inchicore Catholic Club, 1898 (Hoey and Denning
    MSS, parcel 28).
Egan, Michael (ed.). 'Memorials of the dead: Dublin city and county'. Typescript
    of The Ireland branch of the Irish Genealogical Research Soc., 26 Dec. 1988
    (Shelf, 6.1).

National Library of Ireland
Giraldus Cambrensis. *Topographia Hibernica* and *Expugnatio Hiberniae* with illustra-
    tions and map of Ireland. Early thirteenth century (MS 700).
A survey of part of Newtowne and Kilmainham left out of the Phoenix Park by
    making the wall straight measured by Thomas Taylor, 1671 (MS 16. G. 17 (48)).

Press-cuttings by R.D. Walshe [relating to Kilmainham, Dolphin's Barn, Chapelizod and Islandbridge] (MSS 11,655-11,656).
Ordnance survey letters, 1839, from O'Donovan, Curry, etc. (Typescript, Nat. Lib. Ir 9141024. There are also copies in some other libraries).

National Museum
Kilmainham bell (artefact no.1917-2).
Kilmainham brooch (artefact no.45).
Excavations of Gerhard Bersu at the Royal Hospital Kilmainham, 1948 (notebooks and plans).

Public Record Office, Northern Ireland
Interrogatories concerning the common green of Kilmainham: answers of deponents, May 1596 (T.779 (1). Microfilm at Nat. Lib. of Ire. P.363).

Royal Irish Academy
Transcription of the '*Registrum de Kilmainham*' (MS 12 B.1).
Book of Hy Many (MS 1225, 10 (46) vb).

Sovereign Military Hospitaller Order of Malta, Dublin
A guide to St John's House (Clyde Road, Donnybrook, 4). (Typescript).

Trinity College, Dublin
Annals of Ulster (MS 1282, formerly H.1.8).
Annals of Clonmacnoise translated into English AD 1627 by Conell Mageoghagan (MS 673, formerly MS F.3.19).
Transcription of annals in Irish made AD 1734-5 by Hugh O'Molloy (MS 1300/1).
Transcription of annals in Irish made *c.* AD 1764, perhaps by Maurice O'Gorman (MS 1279).

University College Dublin
Wells of Leinster (Folklore Dept., AD 1934-7, MS IFC 468).
St John's Eve (Folklore Dept., AD 1943, MS IFC 959).
Jago, Derek. 'Kilmainham court-house: historical building study for the degree of Master of Urban and Building Conservation'. Thesis, 1991.

PARLIAMENTARY PAPERS

Report of the select committee appointed to inquire into the extent, causes and consequences of the prevailing vice of intoxication among the labouring classes of the United Kingdom, in order to ascertain whether any legislative measures can be devised to prevent the further spread of so great a national evil. H.C., 1834, viii, 315.
Second report of a committee appointed by the secretary of state for war to inquire into the comparative advantages of in-door and out-door pensions for the numbers who can be accommodated at Chelsea and Kilmainham; and generally into the economy of the two establishments; with minutes of evidence. H.C. 1871, xiv, 193.

Evidence and *Report of the royal commission appointed to inquire into the boundaries and municipal areas of certain cities and towns in Ireland.* H.C., 1880, L, 1 and 1880/1, xxx, 327.

Report of the committee appointed to inquire into the royal hospitals at Chelsea and Kilmainham, [etc.]. H.C., 1883, xv, 49.

Report of War Office committee (Lord Belper) on the origin and formation of Chelsea and Kilmainham hospitals, and whether their revenue could be more advantageously used for the benefit of the army; evidence and appx. H.C., 1894, xix, 295.

REFERENCE WORKS AND SOURCE COMPILATIONS

Acta S.S. (*Acta Sanctorum* [etc.]. Ed. Michael Colgan. Antwerp [etc.], 1643-).

AFM (*Annals of the Four Masters.* Ed. and translated by John O'Donovan. Dublin, 1856. Reprinted 1990).

Annals of Clonmacnoise translated into English AD 1627 by Conell Mageoghagan. Ed. D. Murphy. Dublin 1896.

Annals of Loch Cé. Ed. William Hennessy. 2 vols., London, 1871.

Annals of Ulster: a chronicle of Irish affairs AD 431-1540. Ed. William Hennessy. 4 vols, Dublin, 1887.

Annals of Ulster (to AD 1131). Ed. S. MacAirt and G. MacNiocaill. Dublin, 1983.

Ball, *County of Dublin.*

Black's *Bible Dictionary.* 8th ed., 1973.

Cal. anc. rec. Dublin.

Cal. doc. Ire.

Cal. justic. rolls Ire.

Cal. S. P. Ire.

Cambr. ev. (*Cambrensis eversus*, ed. M. Kelly. 3 vols, Dublin, 1848).

Civil Survey, AD 1654-56

Cog. Gaedhel (*Cogadh Gaedhel re Gallaibh: the war of the Gaedhil with the Gaill.* Ed. J.H. Todd. London, 1867).

Commons' Jn. Ire.

De L'Isle & Dudley mss, ii. H. M. C. report, 1934.

Dict. Ir. lang. Ed. Royal Irish Academy.

Extents Ir. mon. possessions.

Fiants Eliz.

Historical and municipal documents of Ireland AD 1172-1320 from the archives of the city of Dublin. Ed. J.T. Gilbert. London, 1870.

Gwynn & Hadcock, *Medieval religious houses in Ireland.*

Hogan, Edmund, *Onomasticon Goedelicum.*

Kenney, James F., *The Sources for the Early History of Ireland: Ecclesiastical.*

Lewis, *Topog. dict. Ire.*

MacMillan's *Encyclopaedia of Religions*

N.H.I. (*New History of Ireland.* Dublin 1968-)

New concise British flora. Ed. W. Keble Martin. 3rd ed., London, 1974

Martyrology of Donegal: a calendar of the saints of Ireland. Translated from the original Irish by the late John O'Donovan, edited with the Irish text, by J. Todd and W. Reeves. Dublin, 1864.

Martyrology of Gorman. Ed. Whitley Stokes. Henry Bradshaw Society, ix, London, 1895.
Martyrology of Oengus ['Felire Oengusso']. Ed. Whitley Stokes. Henry Bradshaw Society, xxix, London, 1905.
Martyrology of Tallaght from the Book of Leinster and MS 5100-4 in The Royal Library, Brussels. Ed. R. Irvine & H. Jackson Lawlor. London, 1931.
MacLysaght, *Ir. life.*
Obits and Martyrology of Christ Church. Ed. J.C. Crosthwaite. Dublin, 1844
O'Hanlon, *Lives* (John O'Hanlon. *Lives of the saints with special festivals, compiled from calendars, martyrologies and various sources.* 11 volumes. Dublin, 1875-[1896]).
Registrum de Kilmainham 1326-39 (Charles McNeill (ed.), *Registrum de Kilmainham 1326-39* (Dublin, 1932)).
Reg. St John Dublin.
Shell guide to Ireland. Ed. Lord Killanin and M.V. Duignan. Revised Dublin, 1969.
Stat. Ire.
Stat. parl. U. K.
S. P. Hen. VIII.
Thom's *Directory.*

ARTICLES AND BOOKS

Aalen, F.H.A. and Whelan, K. *Dublin city and county: from prehistory to present.* Dublin, 1992.
(Alen, John). 'The *Reportorium Viride* of John Alen, Archbishop of Dublin 1533'. In *Anal. Hib.*, x (1941).
Anon. 'Fires of bone'. In *Ulster Jn. Arch.*, vii (1859) and viii (1860).
Anon. 'The bonfires of St John'. In *Cork Hist. Soc. Jn.*, i (1892).
Anon. 'Bell of Kilmainham'. In *R.S.A.I. Jn.*, xxx (1900).
Anon. 'Bully's Acre and body-snatchers'. In *Old Inchicore and Kilmainham: a journal of local history and heritage*, no. 1 (1990).
Alemand, L.A. *Histoire Monastique d'Irlande.* Paris, 1690.
—— *Monasticon Hibernicum.* English version, London, 1722.
Archdall, Mervyn. *Monasticon Hibernicum: the history of the abbies, priories and other religious houses in Ireland.* Dublin, 1786.
Ardagh, John. 'A Dublin statue to Shakespeare'. In *Irish Book Lover*, xv (April 1925).
Ball, F.E. 'St Patrick's Well'. In *R.S.A.I. Jn.*, xxxii (1902).
Barry, James. *Glasnevin Cemetery: a short history of the famous catholic necropolis.* Dublin, 1932.
Bennett, Douglas. *Encyclopaedia of Dublin.* Dublin, 1991.
Best, R.I. 'The Leabhar Oiris'. In *Ériu*, i (1904).
Bok, Johs. *Norse antiquities in Ireland.* Part iii of Haakon Shetelig (ed.), *Viking antiquities in Great Britain and Ireland* (Oslo, 1940).
Bourke, Cormac. 'Early Irish hand-bells'. In *R.S.A.I. Jn.*, cx (1980).
Bradshaw, Brendan. *The dissolution of the religious orders under Henry VIII.* Cambridge, 1974.
—— 'George Browne, first reformation archbishop of Dublin 1536-54'. In *Eccl. Hist. Jn.*, xxi (1970).

Brenneman, Walter and Mary. *Crossing the circle at the holy wells of Ireland.* Virginia, U.S.A., 1995.

Bryce, James. *Geology of Clydesdale and Arran ... and notices of its scenery and antiquities.* London and Glasgow, 1859.

Burke, Nuala. 'A secret church? The structure of Catholic Dublin in the mid-eighteenth century'. In *Arch. Hib.*, xxxii (1974).

Burke, Peter. *Popular culture in early modern Europe.* London, 1978.

Burton, Nathanael. *History of the Royal Hospital Kilmainham.* Dublin, 1843.

Byrne, F.J. *Irish kings and high-kings.* London, 1973.

Cameron, Charles. 'Some recollections of a long life in Dublin'. In *Lady in the House.* Christmas, 1915.

Carrigan, William. *History and antiquity of the Diocese of Ossory.* 4 vols, Dublin 1905.

Chart, D.A. *The story of Dublin.* London, 1907.

Chatterton Newman, Roger. *Brian Boru, King of Ireland.* Dublin, 1983.

Childers, E.S.E. and Stewart, R. *The story of the Royal Hospital Kilmainham.* 2nd. ed., London, 1921.

Clarke, Howard B. 'Gaelic, Viking and Hiberno-Norse Dublin'. In Cosgrove, *Dublin through the ages.*

— *Medieval Dublin: the living city.* Dublin, 1990.

— *Medieval Dublin: the making of a metropolis.* Dublin, 1990.

— 'The Vikings in Ireland: a historian's perspective'. In *Archaeology Ireland,* ix, no. 3 (Autumn, 1995).

Cogan, A. *Diocese of Meath: Ancient and Modern.* 3 vols, Dublin, 1862-70.

Colley, R. *An account of the founding of the Royal Hospital of King Charles II near Dublin* [etc]. Dublin, 1725.

Conaghan, M., Gleeson, O., Maddock, A., (eds). *The Grand Canal: Inchicore and Kilmainham.* Dublin, 1991.

Cooke, Pat. *A history of Kilmainham Gaol.* Dublin, 1995.

Corcoran, Deirdre. 'Goldenbridge cemetery'. In *Old Inchicore and Kilmainham,* no.1 (1990).

Cordner, W.S. 'The cult of the holy well'. In *Ulster Jn. Arch.,* ix (1946).

Corish, P.J. 'The Catholic community in the nineteenth century'. In *Archiv. Hib.,* xxxviii (1983).

Cosgrove, Art. *Dublin through the ages.* Dublin, 1988.

Costello, Murray & Beaumont (ed. John Costello). *An introduction to the Royal Hospital Kilmainham – its architecture, history and restoration.* Dublin, 1987.

Costello, Peter. *Churches of Dublin.* Dublin, 1989.

Craig, Maurice. *The architecture of Ireland from the earliest times to 1880.* London and Dublin, 1982.

Crawford, H.C. 'A descriptive list of early Irish crosses'. In *R.S.A.I. Jn.,* xxxvii (1907).

Crawford, Jon. *Anglicizing the government of Ireland.* Dublin, 1993.

Crofton Croker, T. *Researches in the south of Ireland,* ed. Kevin Danaher. Dublin, 1981.

Cromwell, Thomas. *Excursions through Ireland.* London, 1820.

D'Alton, John. *The history of the county of Dublin.* Dublin, 1838.

— *A memoir of the Great Southern & Western Railway of Ireland.* Dublin, 1846.

Daly, Mary E. *Dublin: the deposed capital.* Cork, 1984.

Danaher, Kevin. 'June'. In *Biatas: the beet grower,* xii (1958).

— *The year in Ireland: Irish calendar customs.* Cork, 1972.

Davies, Wendy. 'The place of healing in early Irish society'. In Ó Corráin et al., *Sages, saints and storytellers.*

De L. Smyth, J. *A site for the new university: a plea for the Royal Hospital Kilmainham.* Dublin, [1908].

de Courcy, Seán. 'Looking at the Liffey in 795'. In *Archaeology Ireland*, ix, no. 3 (Autumn, 1995).

De Paor, Liam and Máire. *Early Christian Ireland.* 3rd ed., London, 1961.

Dixon Hardy, Philip. *The holy wells of Ireland.* Dublin, 1836.

Donnelly, N. *History of Dublin parishes.* Dublin, 1909.

Eames, Elizabeth and Fanning, Tom. *Irish medieval tiles.* Dublin, 1988.

Ellis, Steven. *Tudor Ireland: crown, community and the conflict of cultures 1470-1603.* Dublin, 1985.

— *Reform and revival: English government in Ireland 1470-1534.* Suffolk, 1986.

Fagan, Patrick. *The second city: portrait of Dublin 1700-1760.* Dublin, 1986.

Falkiner, C.L. 'The Phoenix Park, its origin and early history, with some notices of its royal and viceregal residents'. In *R.I.A. Proc.,* vi (1900-2).

— 'The Hospital of St John of Jerusalem in Ireland'. In *R.I.A. Proc.,* xxvi, sec.C (1907).

'Fingal', 'The Liffey from its source to Poolbeg'. In *Ir. Builder,* xxv (1883).

Fitzsimons, Marie. 'Prior John Rawson and the dissolution of Kilmainham'. In *Old Inchicore and Kilmainham,* no.2 (1963).

Flower, Robin. *Catalogue of Irish MSS in British Museum.* 3 vols., London, 1926.

Gribben, Arthur. *Holy wells and sacred water sources in Britain and Ireland: an annotated bibliography.* New York and London, 1992.

— 'Bishops of Dublin'. Reprinted from *Rep.Nov.,* i (1955-6), pp 1-26 in Clarke, *Medieval Dublin: the living city.*

Gwynn, Aubrey, *The Irish church in the eleventh and twelfth centuries,* ed. Gerard O'Brien. Dublin, 1992.

Gwynn, E.J. and Purton, W.J. 'The monastery of Tallaght'. In *R.I.A. Proc.,* xxix (1912).

Haliday, Charles. *Scandinavian kingdom of Dublin.* 2nd ed., Dublin, 1884.

Harbison, Peter. *The high crosses of Ireland: an iconographical and photographic survey.* 3 vols, Bonn, 1992.

Harris, Walter. *The history and antiquities of the city of Dublin.* Dublin and London, 1766.

Healy, John. 'The monastic school of St Enda of Aran' in his *Insula sanctorum et doctorum or Ireland's ancient schools and scholars.* Dublin, 1890.

Healy, Paddy. 'Con Colbert Road, Inchicore Nth.'. In *Excavations 1989.*

Hennessy, Mark. 'The priory and hospital of Newgate: the evolution and decline of a medieval monastic estate'. In *Common Ground* (1988).

Henry, Françoise. 'Early Christian slabs and pillar stones in the West of Ireland'. In *R.S.A.I. Jn.,* lxvii (1937).

Heraughty, Patrick. *Inishmurray: ancient monastic island.* Dublin, 1982.

Higgins, J.G. *The early Christian cross slabs, pillar stones and related monuments of County Galway.* 2 vols, B.A.R. International Series 375, Oxford, 1987.

Hughes, Kathleen. *The Church in early Irish society.* London, 1966.

Hurley, Shay. 'St Michael's C.B.S., Keogh Square and Richmond Barracks recalled'. In *Old Inchicore and Kilmainham,* no.1 (1990).

Igoe, Vivien, and O'Dwyer, Fred. 'Early views of the Royal Hospital, Kilmainham'. In *The GPA Irish Arts Review*. Dublin, 1988.

Jacob, William. 'Kingsbridge Terminus'. In *D. H. R.*, vi (1944).

Keenahan, Peter. 'The Shakespeare House, Old Kilmainham'. In *Old Inchicore and Kilmainham*, no.2 (1993).

Kelly, Frieda. *A history of Kilmainham Gaol: the dismal house of little ease*. Cork, 1988.

Kendrick, T.D. *The Druids*. London, 1927.

Kennedy, Evory. *On the neglect of sanitary arrangements in the homes and houses of the rich and poor in town and county*. Dublin, 1865.

Kenny, Colum. 'The Four Courts in Dublin before 1796'. In *Ir. Jurist*, n.s. xxi (1986).

— 'Paradox or pragmatist? "Honest Tristram Kennedy" (1805-85): lawyer, educationalist, land agent and member of parliament'. In *R.I.A. Proc.*, xcii (1992).

Kermode, P.M.C. *Manx crosses*. London, 1907.

Kilmainham Jail Restoration Society. *Ghosts of Kilmainham*. Dublin, 1963.

— *Kilmainham: the Bastille of Ireland*. Rev. ed., Dublin, 1982.

Lennon, Colm. *Sixteenth century: the incomplete conquest*. Dublin, 1994.

Lennox Barrow, G. 'The Knights Hospitallers of St John of Jerusalem at Kilmainham'. In *D. H. R.*, xxxviii (1985).

[L'Estrange, Joseph] 'Brasspen'. 'John's Well in the olden time: a sketch from real life'. In *Salmagundi*, xxii (5 July 1834). The author is identified at John McCall, 'Joseph L'Estrange ('Brasspen'): memoir of a forgotten writer' in *The Irish Emerald*, ii, no.2 (3 Sept. 1892), p. 839.

Lynch, Geraldine. 'The holy wells of County Wicklow: traditions and legends'. In K. Hannigan and W. Nolan (eds), *Wicklow: history and society* (Dublin, 1994).

MacCana, Pronsias. *Celtic mythology*. London, 1970.

MacGiolla Phádraig, Brian. 'Dr John Carpenter: archbishop of Dublin 1760-1786'. In *D. H. R.*, xxx, no.1 (December, 1976).

MacNeill, Máire. *The festival of Lughnasa: a study of the survival of the Celtic festival of the beginning of the harvest*. Dublin, 1982.

Mac Thomáis, Éamonn. *Me jewel and darlin' Dublin*. New ed., Dublin, 1994.

McGregor, J. *Picture of Dublin*. Dublin, 1821.

McGuirk, Phyllis. 'St Michael's Church, Inchicore'. In *Old Inchicore and Kilmainham*, no.2 (1993).

McNamara, Martin. 'Psalter text and Psalter study in the early Irish church (AD 600-1200)'. In *R.I.A. Proc.*, lxxiii (1973).

McNeill, Charles. 'The Hospitallers at Kilmainham and their guests'. In *R.S.A.I. Jn.*, liv (1924).

— 'Hospital of St John without the Newgate, Dublin'. Reprinted from *R.S.A.I. Jn.*, lv (1925) in Clarke, *Medieval Dublin: the living city*.

— 'Report on recent acquisitions in the Bodleian Library, Oxford' [since 1916]. In *Anal. Hib.*, i (1930).

Malcolm, Elizabeth. *'Ireland sober, Ireland free': drink and temperance in nineteenth-century Ireland*. Dublin, 1986

Meyer, Kuno (ed.). *The Triads of Ireland*. R.I.A. Todd Lecture Series, xiii, Dublin, 1906.

Meyler, Walter. *St Catherine's Bells: an autobiography*. 2 vols, London and Dublin, 1868-70.

Mills, James. 'The Norman settlement in Leinster: the cantreds near Dublin'. In *R.S.A.I., Jn.*, xxiv (1894).

Minahane, John. 'The knights of Kilmainham'. In *Old Inchicore and Kilmainham*, no.1 (1990).

Moody, T.W. and Martin, F.X. (eds). *The Course of Irish History*. Revised and enlarged ed., Dublin, 1994.

Mould, Daphe Pochin. *The Irish saints*. Dublin and London, 1964.

Murphy, Séan (ed.). *Bully's Acre and Royal Hospital Kilmainham graveyards: history and inscriptions*. Dublin, 1989.

Neary, John. 'Pilgrimages to sacred wells'. In *I.E.R,* 5th.s., xxvii (1926).

Nowlan, A.J. 'Kilmainham Jail'. In *D.H.R.*, xv (1960).

O'Brien, Elizabeth. 'A tale of two cemeteries'. In *Archaeology Ireland*, ix, no.3 (Autumn, 1995).

O'Broin, Sean. *The book of Finglas*. Dublin, 1980.

O'Connor, Charles (ed.). *Rerum Hibernicarum Scriptores*. London 1826.

Ó Corráin, D. et al. (eds), *Sages, saints and storytellers: Celtic studies in honour of Professor James Carney*. Maynooth, 1989.

O'Curry, Eugene. *Lectures on the manuscript materials of ancient Irish history*. Dublin, 1861, reprinted 1995.

— *On the manners and customs of the ancient Irish*. 3 vols., London, 1873.

Ó Danachair, Caoimhín. 'The holy wells of Co. Dublin'. In *Report. Nov.*, ii, no.1 (1958) and ii, no.2 (1960).

— 'Holy well legends in Ireland'. In *Saga och sed* (1959).

O'Dea, L. 'The Hospitals of Kilmainham'. In *D. H. R.*, xx (1965).

O'Donovan, J. (ed.), *The book of rights: Leabhar na gCeart*. Dublin, 1847.

O'Dwyer, Peter. *Céli Dé: spiritual reform in Ireland 750-900*. 2nd. ed., Dublin, 1981.

O'Grady, Standish (ed.). *Silva Gadelica: a collection of tales in Irish edited from manuscripts and translated*. 2 vols, London, 1892.

Ó hOgain, Daithi. *Myth, Legend and Romance: an encyclopaeia of the Irish folk tradition*. New York, 1991.

O'Keeffe, Peter and Sinnington, Tom. *Irish stone bridges: history and heritage*. Dublin, 1991.

Olley, John. 'Sustaining the narrative at Kilmainham'. In *Irish Arts Review: yearbook 1991-2*. Dublin, 1991.

Ó Maitiú, Seamús. *The humours of Donnybrook: Dublin's famous fair and its suppression*. Dublin, 1995.

O'Meara, John J. (ed.).*Topography of Ireland by Giraldus Cambrensis*. Rev. ed., London, 1982.

Omont, Henri. *Catalogue des Manuscrits Celtiques et Basques de la Bibliothèque Nationale*. Paris, 1890.

O'Neill, John (ed.). *The Well: newsletter of Samyedzong Buddhist Centre and the community associated with Kilmainham Well House*, i, nos 1 & 2. Dublin, 1995.

O'Rahilly, T.F. *Early Irish history and mythology*. Dublin, 1976.

O'Reily, M.A.J. 'The historical background of Garda headquarters, Kilmainham'. In *Garda Review* (April 1941).

Ó Riain, Padraig. *Corpus Genealogiarum Sanctorum Hiberniae*. Dublin, 1985.

Price, Liam. *Place-names of Wicklow, v*. Dublin, 1957, reprinted 1983.

Richter, Michael. *Medieval Ireland: the enduring tradition*. Dublin, 1988.

Rocque, John. *Plan of the city of Dublin and the environs*. Dublin, 1756.

Ronan, Myles. *The Reformation in Dublin*. London, 1926.

Ryan, John. *Irish monasticism: origins and early development*. Dublin, 1931 and 1972 (new introduction and bibliography).

— 'Pre-Norman Dublin'. In *R.S.A.I. Jn., lxxix* (1949).

Rynne, Etienne. 'Excavation of a church-site at Clondalkin, Co.Dublin'. In *R.S.A.I. Jn*, xcvii (1967).

[Seaton, B.M.] *The Kilmainham Pensioner's Lament*. Dublin, 1834.

Sharpe, Richard. 'Some problems concerning the organisation of the church in early medieval Ireland'. In *Peritia*, iii (1984).

— 'Quatuor sanctissimi episcopi: Irish saints before St Patrick'. In Ó Corráin, *Sages, saints and storytellers*.

— *Medieval Irish saint's lives: an introduction to vitae sanctorum Hiberniae*. Oxford, 1991.

Sheehy, Jeanne. *Kingsbridge Station*. Dublin, 1973.

Sheehy, Maurice. *Discovering the Dingle area using your feet*. Tralee, 1979.

— *Motorists guide to the Dingle peninsula*. [Tralee] 1993.

Smyth, Alfred P. *Scandinavian York and Dublin*. Dublin, 1979.

St John Joyce, Weston. *The neighbourhood of Dublin*. Dublin, 1912.

Staples, Hugh (ed.). *The Ireland of Sir Jonah Barrington: selections from his personal sketches*. London, 1967.

Stokes, Whitley (ed.). *Three Irish glossaries*. London, 1862.

— *Lives of the saints from the Book of Lismore*. Oxford, 1980.

Stuart, James. *Historical memoirs of the city of Armagh*. Newry, 1819.

Stuart, T.P. 'Kilmainham: the Royal Hospital and its predecessors there'. In *Lady in the House* (Christmas, 1922).

Sweeney, Clair. *Rivers of Dublin*. Dublin, 1991.

Todd, J.H. 'Report on Irish MSS preserved in the Royal Library, Paris'. In *R.I.A. Proc.*, iii (1847).

Vigors, Philip. 'Query re the term 'Merry Gallons' yearly levied off the inhabitants and tenants of Kilmainham. Answered by Sylvester Malone'. In *R.S.A.I. Jn.*, xii (1902).

Wakeman, W.P. 'Inis Muiredach, now Inis[h]murray, and its antiquities'. In *Royal Hist. and Arch. Association of Ireland*, 4th. s., vii (1885-6).

Walker, Joseph. 'Memoir on the armour and weapons of the Irish'. In his *Historical memoirs* (Dublin, 1786).

Warburton, J., Whitelaw, J., and Walsh, R., *History of the city of Dublin*. 2 vols, London, 1818.

Ware, James. *Antiquities of Ireland*. 1st. ed., Latin, London, 1654 and accurate English translation, Dublin, 1705

Ware, James. 'Antiquities' in *Works concerning Ireland, revised and improved*. Ed. W. Harris. 2 vols., Dublin, 1739 and 1745.

Weir, Anthony. *Early Ireland: a field guide*. Belfast, 1980.

Went, A.E.J. 'Fisheries of the River Liffey'. Reprinted from *R.S.A.I. Jn.*, lxxxiii (1953) in Clarke, *Medieval Dublin: the living city*.

Wilkinson, George. *Practical geology and ancient architecture in Ireland*. London and Dublin, 1845.

Wood, Herbert. 'The Templars in Ireland'. In *R.I.A. Proc.*, xxvi (1906-7).

Woods, James. *Annals of Westmeath: ancient and modern*. Dublin, 1907.

Wright, G.N. *Historical guide to Dublin*. 2nd ed., Dublin, 1825.

Indexes

Footnotes in main text may be consulted for further references

INDEX OF PERSONS

INDEX OF PLACES

SELECT GENERAL INDEX